# The Harvard Mystique

THE
# HARVARD
The Power Syndrome
from Sesame Street

ENRIQUE HANK LOPEZ

# MYSTIQUE

That Affects Our Lives
to the White House

MACMILLAN PUBLISHING CO., INC.

New York

Copyright©1979 by Enrique Hank Lopez

Macmillan Publishing Co., Inc.
866 Third Avenue, New York, N.Y. 10022
Collier Macmillan Canada, Ltd.

Library of Congress Cataloging in Publication Data

Lopez, Enrique Hank.
    The Harvard mystique.

    1. Harvard University—Alumni. 2. Power (Social
sciences) 3. Elite (Social sciences) I. Title.
LD2142.L66    378.744′4    79-14
ISBN 0-02-575120-4

First Printing 1979
Printed in the United States of America

# Contents

# Foreword

MACHIAVELLI, resurrected, would instantly understand the bottom-line bearing of *The Harvard Mystique:* present-day political power and its manifold ramifications on the international and domestic scenes. But a reincarnated Plato and Aristotle would be more than a little bemused. This ultimate realization of their respective *Akademeia* and *Lykeion* as a sprawling intellectual stadium and supermarket on the River Charles in Cambridge, Massachusetts, would no doubt lead them to some deep brooding.

Probably to most Americans Harvard is the name of an effete college at which some 1,200 upper-class youths enroll each year after completing high school or private prep school, there to pass four years desultorily studying, engaging in horseplay and possibly becoming incidentally contaminated with outlandish notions instilled by pink professors bearing bizarre names. But, wrong though this hinterland conception may be, the undergraduate college is the least of what the author is concerned about. This happens to be the case even though a minority of the collegians in final receipt of the coveted *cum laude, magna cum laude* and *summa cum laude* provides the recruits for postgraduate specialization either at one of Harvard's numerous graduate schools or at some dozen or two institutional emulators scattered across the country. Although not enveloped by the mystique of Harvard, these quasi-counterparts have much of the essential muscle—in some areas more.

In the perspective raised by Mr. Lopez, what Harvard really is most basically is a multinational academic conglomerate atop an educational department store and supermarket, plus a think tank to outrank all think tanks—the whole supported by a deftly managed $1.5 billion investment trust. And the word "academic" should put no one off. For Harvard is, among other things, a producer of special techniques of control, ideas, theories, programs and above all of specially trained personnel—all of direct multifaceted service to government at home and to friendly foreign governments; to corporations, banks and insurance companies; to public school systems and to special schools and other universities; and to hospitals, clinics, the established professions and so on *ad infinitum*. With respect to this melange the Harvard watchword of *Veritas* takes on many colors and shadings.

It is to give some idea of the impact on the contemporary world of some of this area that Mr. Lopez has cast a good-humored, informal but fairly systematic and surely knowledgeable eye over the place, at the same time getting into some of the major controversies, minor bickerings, infighting and scuttlebutt peculiar to the subject. He also wrestles mightily with the national image of Harvard, a brooding presence, which is to some extent publicly exaggerated and misplaced as in the case of most institutional images.

Being first on the ground, and with Yankee foresight usually keeping pace with developments, at times a step or two ahead of them, it has to this date produced more professionals and more high government officials of every stripe—including presidents, diplomats and Supreme Court justices—than any other American institution of higher learning. That in itself has given it extra mention in many contexts far from its environs. It is true, though, as the author stresses, that the media appear systematically to mention the Harvard connection of public figures and fail to note the university connection of most others. This seeming media partiality is annoying to many non-Harvardians.

Why do the media comport themselves as they do? To this conundrum I may suggest a solution. For one thing, Harvard—as we have seen, a very old institution—although not the largest in volume of students is foremost in prestige and financial endowment, and owns most laurels by reason of its long past and of having been the first in so many respects. It was, for example, first of American higher institutions of learning, as far back as the 1840s, to turn from exclusive concern with the classics and the traditional professions and to aggressively embrace and promote science. It was the first to establish specialized graduate schools and has managed to remain first in quality of most of these schools in the judgment of its peers. So, it is *numero uno,* which in itself carries weight in the American psyche. And the media, not altogether obtuse, know this.

The alert newsman, realizing that at Harvard there is an institution thrashing around with all the ingredients of the future astounding discoveries, like Cotton Mather wrestling with the devil, knows that a phone call to its public relations department is pretty certain to lead to quick contact with someone who is *au courant.* In acknowledgment, Harvard is mentioned in news stories—and mentioned and mentioned. A similar call to many other highly rated institutions would not as surely produce the desired information.

Nevertheless and despite all this, as Mr. Lopez brings out very well, there is much solid substance on the complex scene at Harvard, enough to justify the governments of the United States, Saudi Arabia, Japan, Iran, China and a few others to keep in intimate touch with it and, what is more, give it substantial funding. For Harvard probably has more experts or help, ready to spring into action on many fronts, than any other university in the world. There is the same sort of connection with corporations, to all of which the Harvard School of Business Administration is a veritable Mecca.

What Mr. Lopez is concerned to scrutinize, it seems to me, is not the locus of actual power in the modern world, but the seedlings and underpinnings of that power in their forcing ground. In doing this he has directed attention in a new way to a social complex that should give many readers a better background for understanding some of the events that take place from day to day.

Francis Bacon in an oft-quoted maxim said: "Knowledge is power." Bacon had uppermost in mind man's power of dealing with his natural environment. But as this book shows, Bacon's maxim is readily extendable to embrace political and economic power—and personal power. The road to such power in the modern world leads not merely through the marketplace, the political arena or the battlefield, but, first and foremost, through the modern university, whether it is called Harvard or something else. If the battle of Waterloo was won on the playing fields of Eton (which many doubt), it is nevertheless a fact that modern battles take over and diplomatic coups are won or lost on the campuses of the big universities, of which Harvard in the United States is the paradigm, the magnified American version of Oxford and Cambridge rolled into one.

FERDINAND LUNDBERG
Author of *The Rich and The Super Rich*

# Acknowledgments

THERE HAVE BEEN MANY PEOPLE who have offered advice, encouragement and specific information for this book, and I am particularly grateful for the help offered by the following members of the Harvard faculty: Robert Freed Bales, John Kenneth Galbraith, Don K. Price, Jerome Bruner, Harvey Liebenstein, Jerry Lesser, Burton White, Jean Chall, Jonathan Beckwith, and John Charles Haar. I also wish to acknowledge the valuable contributions of Professor John Howard, Professor Mary Howard, Professor Rodolfo Alvarez, McGeorge Bundy, Professors Mathilda and Frank Holzman, Dean John O'Byrne, Mary and Jerry Wenig, Sander Johnson, John Hopkins, Ted Brown and Caldwell Colt. There are several writers whose books and articles have provided me with additional insights and information, among whom are Ralph Blumenfeld, Patricia Linden, David Halberstam, E. J. Kahn and Arthur Jensen. I have also had the benefit of source material from *The New York Times, The New York Post, The Washington Post, Time, Newsweek, Atlantic Monthly, Harper's* and several other newspapers and magazines.

I am most particularly grateful for the help and advice of my old and esteemed friend Ferdinand Lundberg, who is most knowledgeable about the sources and uses of power and wealth. And my belated thanks to Beatrice Spencer for her help with the manuscript.

# The Harvard Mystique

Flaherty reached for another folder, flipped it open, and handed Monckton a paper. "That's the biography on one of the three present Commissioners. He is the top candidate for Chairman."

"Shit, Frank! Look here. He's another Harvard. Went in as a Curry appointment. Don't your little personnel boys understand what we're trying to do, Frank? Can't we find a tough bastard who is for us? Maybe a graduate of Tulane or Kansas State or Illinois? Take this bastard off the list, Frank, and never again, *never* again bring me a name from Harvard. And no more Curry holdovers. They are out. Understood, Frank? *Out!*"

Excerpt from *The Company*
John Ehrlichman's novel
about the Nixon White House

# Introduction

MANY YEARS AGO, during my senior year at the University of Denver, I was faced with the happy dilemma of choosing between Harvard, Yale, Columbia or the University of California at Berkeley, each of which had granted me a fellowship for graduate study in economics. Since I was then a houseguest of S.I. Hayakawa, for whom the university had provided a four-bedroom mansion during his stint as professor of general semantics for the summer session, I naturally asked his advice.

"Well," he said after a long meditative pause, "I guess you should go to Harvard. Then you won't be bugged by that mystique. Theoretically, I should be immune to the impact of any label or symbol, but that Harvard label has always bothered me. Something happens to me when I'm in the presence of a Harvard man—I sort of lose my confidence, even though I know some of them are really stupid asses. So if you go there, Hank, you wont't be so easily taken in by all that Harvard crap."

The following day I posed the same question to my favorite professor, Dr. Robert Woolbert, who had received his doctorate

[1]

(with highest honors) from Harvard. Without a moment's
hesitation, he said, "Harvard, of course."

"Why?" I asked. "Just because you've been there?"

"Not at all," he said. "I just think you ought to go there
because Harvard is the fountain of all bullshit—but you can't say
that unless you've been there."

In essence, both of them were saying the same thing from
different perspectives. And, needless to say, the university
frequently gets more credit than it deserves and just as frequently
gets more criticism than is justified. But no matter what is said or
written about it, whether high praise or brutal damnation, the
Harvard mystique persists with a sort of self-nourishing
stamina—and its influence is perhaps most pervasive among
people who have never been to Cambridge. For example, a year
ago I hired four students to conduct some research that might
offer a quantitative measure of this so-called mystique. I asked
them to review every news article in *The New York Times* for a
period of four months (excluding sports and society items) and
to add up the number of times a university was mentioned in
connection with some individual. Several weeks later they
informed me, with more than a hint of astonishment, that
Harvard had been mentioned three times as often as all other
universities combined.

One might conclude that the *Times* is inordinately affected by
the Harvard mystique, but the same syndrome seems to have
affected most national magazines (*Time, Newsweek, Life, Look,
The New Yorker, The Nation, Harper's, Atlantic Monthly, New
Republic*) and the television network news departments. Indeed,
during the Senate Watergate hearings, millions of TV viewers
were constantly reminded by the commentators that Senator
Sam Ervin, Senator Gurley, Sam Dash and Terry Lenzer were
graduates of the Harvard Law School, but no mention was made
of the law schools attended by Senators Inouye, Talmadge,
Weicker, Baker, Montoya or any other staff counsel. During that
same period the press and broadcast media periodically alluded to

the Harvard antecedents of Archibald Cox, Elliot Richardson, William Ruckelshaus, James St. Clair, Richard Kleindienst, Daniel Ellsberg, and Elizabeth Holtzman—but the public was seldom, if ever, informed of the university connections of Richard Nixon, John Mitchell, H.R. Haldeman, John Ehrlichman, John Dean, Jeb McGruder, Maurice Stans, Gordon Liddy or Howard Hunt.

Interestingly enough, none of the television network anchormen, nor any of their Watergate correspondents, are graduates of Harvard, so that one cannot say they were simply being loyal to their alma mater. When asked about the newscasters' frequent and occasionally awed references to Harvard, one of the more popular anchormen somewhat defensively explained that "you can't escape the symbolic force of that institution. For example, when you mention Henry Kissinger, you almost automatically think about his ties to Harvard—and that was also true of Roosevelt, Kennedy, Acheson, Frankfurter and a lot of other public figures."

Needless to say, many people resent Harvard men, and sometimes their resentment veers toward hatred, which often provokes harsh accusations: "They're a bunch of damned snobs....They're always throwing their weight around.... They're too clannish and exclusive....They're downright incestuous...."

In quite a number of cases such accusations are at least partially justified. For example, thousands of brilliant law school graduates have been turned away by prestigious law firms dominated by Harvard lawyers who seldom hire anyone who has not been schooled in Cambridge. An increasing number of business and industrial conglomerates have shown a distinct preference for graduates of the Harvard Business School. Certain government agencies (in both Republic and Democratic administrations) have been filled with Harvard men in crucial policymaking echelons. University faculties and charitable foundations are often dominated by graduates of Harvard, and they frequently seem somewhat incestuous in their employment of higher-level personnel.

Anyone who visits Cambridge will soon detect the initial symptoms of this academic incest, which can be one of the more amusing aspects of the community. But it is far overshadowed by something else which pervades every facet of that legendary institution—a sense of power, an all-encompassing power that radiates from Harvard and spreads across the country and throughout several continents like an invisible blanket. In the words of a Chinese diplomat-scholar who did his graduate work in the department of economics, "This university is one of the real power centers of the world."

On any given day of the school year, undergraduate and graduate students may attend extra lectures or seminars by visiting scholars, artists, writers and/or public officials whose names are often in the headlines, men and women who readily accept invitations to Harvard because it's considered a prestigious forum. Indeed, some of the students become jaded by what one senior characterized as "this excess of big-shot egomaniacs." On the other hand, some students are chronically attracted to such distinguished visitors and flock after them like campus groupies. "We have a name for that kind of person," a sophomore recently told us. "We call them star-fuckers."

Whatever one may choose to call them, there are some students who undoubtedly come to Harvard because it represents power and influence. Others are drawn by its academic excellence, or because of family pressures, or by the cultural and social ambience of Cambridge, to name but a few of the university's many attractions. As for those who hope to enhance their own personal quest for power, one can detect varying degrees of ambition within the different branches of the university. Most of the undergraduates seem to be concerned with intellectual attainment; whereas most of the graduate students are frankly in pursuit of career advancement.

For example, in personal interviews with a hundred law

students, we learned that 72% were mainly interested in professional success and power, with intellectual excellence a secondary consideration. Among business school students that percentage rose to 85%, while medical students registered 68%. Needless to say, professional students in all other universities probably reflect the same degrees of ambition. In any event, power and influence are among the dominant features of the Cambridge community.

In most instances, "Harvard power" is an obliquely subtle force that functions at subterranean levels, but on certain occasions it flares to the surface as if to remind everyone of its omnipresence. Commenting on this unique phenomenon, Professor John Kenneth Galbraith recently advised us not to ignore "the lucky accident of geographic location" as a principal factor in Harvard's access to governmental influence. "You've got to remember," he said, "that our main thrust in Washington began during the New Deal, when we were traveling on trains rather than planes. Consequently, it was very convenient for us to hop on an overnight sleeper at 8:00 p.m., have a couple of drinks and dinner and get a good night's sleep before arriving in the capital at 7:00 a.m., fully rested and ready for all-day meetings. Then we'd grab another sleeper back to Boston that same evening. But if you were from Yale, you would have to wait till 11:00 or 12:00 midnight to board that sleeper, and you might have to sit up all night because all the Pullman berths would be occupied. If you were a government egghead from Columbia University, you would be boarding a sleeper way after midnight or you could have to take a daylight train and sacrifice a whole day to mere travel. And if your base was Chicago, Ann Arbor or any other midwestern campus, you would be traveling twenty-four hours to get to Washington. Worse yet, if you were one of those brilliant professor-consultants from Berkeley, you would travel three days cross-country for a one-day meeting at some government agency, then take another three days getting back.

"So, as you can easily see, it was easier and cheaper for the

New Deal people to call on a Harvard man for high-caliber. gobbledygook. And by the time plane travel became popular, we had already established firm beachheads in every echelon of the Washington establishment."

With the onset of the jet age, the Harvard power syndrome was soon felt in all corners of the globe. For example, in the late summer of 1969, Professor Wassily Leontief encountered a former student in the vast waiting room of the airport at Rio de Janeiro. "May I ask what you're doing here, professor?" asked the ex-student, now a high-ranking diplomat from Nigeria.

"Just consulting with a few government officials," said Leontief with characteristic modesty. "They seem to be interested in my input-output analysis. But, of course, Brazil has its special problems with this sudden massive input of American dollars and Japanese yen, and perhaps not enough technical expertise to deal with all this overnight expansion. There's such a thing as growing too fast, you know."

Whether or not Brazil entirely accepted Professor Leontief's precautions remains to be seen; but certain other countries in Scandinavia and Western Europe (plus the World Bank and United Nations) have eagerly adopted his input-output budgeting, a complicated statistical technique for analyzing both the anatomy and the physiology of a nation's economy. Beyond its value as a tool of description, it is valuable as a device for prediction and for planning.

Small wonder that Professor Leontief was awarded the Nobel Prize for Economics in 1973, being the fourth Harvard economist to win the prize in four successive years.

But as his colleague, Paul A. Samuelson, recently commented: "The supreme compliment came when the USSR decided that input-output is okay and, like the wireless, is really a Russian invention after all. Since Leontief was part of the earlier wave of Russian emigrant scientists who have enriched American scholarship, this nationalistic predating of the record is harmless enough."

It should be noted that both of these Nobel laureates are what we choose to call *neo-Harvard* men, first members of their respective families to attend the university. The *proto-Harvard* man is one whose ancestors attended Harvard, people like Franklin D. Roosevelt, Robert Lowell, McGeorge Bundy and Henry Adams. Among the most distinguished "neo" graduates are Henry Kissinger, Sam Ervin, Norman Mailer, Felix Frankfurter, Thomas ("Tommy the Cork") Corcoran and John F. Kennedy. As we shall attempt to prove in subsequent chapters of this book, a neo-Harvard man will find an easier path to success in public affairs or private enterprise if he first of all acquires a proto-Harvard man as his mentor or sponsor. And we should also note that some neos lust after proto status with unseemly fervor, often adopting the accent and *modus vivendi* of the old Cantabrigian with rather mixed success.

Some neo-Harvard men seemingly continue to be awed by the protos long after they themselves have achieved great success. Take, for example, Norman Mailer's first-person account of the night he introduced the grandson of the tenth president of Harvard at a peace rally:

Mailer now cranked up a vaudeville clown for finale to Lowell's introduction. "Ladies and gentlemen, if novelists come from the middle class, poets tend to derive from the bottom and the top. We all know good poets at the bot'—ladies and gentlemen, here is a poet from the top, Mr. Robert Lowell." A large vigorous hand of applause, genuine enthusiasm for Lowell, some standing ovation.

But Mailer was depressed. He had betrayed himself again. The end of the introduction belonged in a burlesque house—he worked his own worst veins, like a man on the edge of bankruptcy trying to collect hopeless debts. He was fatally vulgar! Lowell passing him on the stage had recovered sufficiently to cast him a nullifying look. At this moment, they were obviously far from friends.

Lowell's shoulders had a slump, his modest stomach was pushed forward a hint, his chin was dropped to his chest as he stood at the microphone, pondering for a moment. One did not achieve the languid grandeurs of that slouch in one generation—the grandsons of the first sons had best go through the best troughs in the best eating clubs at Harvard before anyone in the family could try for such elegant note. It was now apparent to Mailer that Lowell would move by instinct, ability, and certainly by choice, in the direction most opposite from himself.

"Well," said Lowell softly to the audience, his voice dry and gentle as any New England executioner might ever hope to be, "this has been a zany evening." Laughter came back, perhaps a little too much. It was as if Lowell wished to reprove Mailer, not humiliate him....His firmness, his distaste for the occasion, communicated some subtle but impressive sense of his superiority.

Commenting on this passage from *The Armies of the Night,* one of Mailer's oldest friends told me that he had always suspected that Mailer had been severely traumatized by his undergraduate experience at Harvard. "That was Norman's first exposure to the power elite," his friend theorized. "And, as a middle-class Jew from Brooklyn, he probably felt like a rank outsider—snubbed, ignored and put down by all those super-secure preppies from Groton, Exeter, Choate, and St. Paul's. That's probably why he has written so damned little about his four years in Cambridge: they were probably too painful, too bitter. But when (and if) Mailer finally decides to write about that period, it should be explosive...or embarrassingly maudlin."

My former law partner Sander, a middle-class Swede from North Dakota, would undoubtedly sympathize with Mailer's reactions to the so-called Brahmins at Harvard. He sat next to Elliot Richardson in a class on equity at the law school, and Richardson never said a word to Sander during the entire course, not even a simple reciprocal "good morning." But at the very end of the last lecture, when the entire class was standing and applauding the professor, Richardson turned to Sander and said, "I say, old man, I'm sorry we've never been introduced—but it's been awfully nice sitting next to you."

Such "shyness" or social reticence seems less prevalent among current students at Harvard, and Richardson himself apparently became more accessible as a public figure of considerable distinction. In any event, whenever he or any other Harvard man is mentioned in the press, radio or television—with an occasional reference to his university affiliation—the so-called Harvard mystique is inevitably (though perhaps imperceptibly) enhanced in the public mind. But one might logically ask, how much of this mystique is mere puffery, a bloated reputation that feeds on itself? Or is that reputation based on a continuing record of achievement by the faculty and graduates of the university?

And if the answer to the latter question is affirmative, one must then ask if Harvard itself produces powerful men and women or merely attracts people who would have been powerful anyway—power attracting power, just as money attracts money. By what mysterious process does the university select the chosen few from the thousands who apply for admission—and what does it do for those who are accepted? For example:

Would Henry Kissinger have been secretary of state if he had been from Michigan University instead of Harvard?

Would B. F. Skinner's theories have created a universal furor if he were a professor at Denver University instead of Harvard?

Would John Kenneth Galbraith be so highly regarded by the press if he were teaching at the University of Texas?

Obviously, there are too many variables and contingencies in all of these questions, so that no clear answers can be given, but they do provide a fascinating field of inquiry and conjecture.

On a recent visit to Cambridge, I posed some of these questions to several first-year students, and one of them simply shrugged with a certain weary insouciance: "You're always reading or hearing about some Harvard man fucking things up and getting praised for doing it fancy."

Accepting that skeptical stance as a *modus operandi*, I have undertaken an in-depth investigation and analysis of Harvard's present-day influence in government, politics, law, business, economics, the communications media, publishing, entertainment, education, the fine arts, literature and even *Sesame Street.* Some readers may eventually agree with the disgruntled southern senator who said he was "goddam sick and tired of Harvard and all them snobs that come from up there, including Sam Ervin. And now even Johnny Carson has swallowed their crap and starts raving about Harvard, just because a bunch of smart-ass kids invited him up to Cambridge and gave him some kind of lampoon."

Two more recent events revealed more positive attitudes about the university—and each, in its own way, contributed to the Harvard mystique:

The first was Justice Lewis Powell's landmark decision in the Bakke case, where he specifically noted Harvard's "flexible" way of considering race as one criterion for admission. Although several other schools have similar procedures, he mentioned only Harvard, and the national media immediately emphasized this fact. In its cover story on the decision, *Time* magazine ran a separate, prominently displayed article titled "Harvard's Way," in which the college's multiple-criteria system was explained at length. (More on this in Chapter I.) "But why did Powell single out Harvard?" asked an irate Columbia professor. "You'd think those people in Cambridge invented race-awareness....and everything else."

The second event was Aleksandr Solzhenitsyn's commencement address to the class of '78, which lured scores of reporters to Cambridge. His negative appraisal of Western society was widely publicized throughout the free world; and almost without exception, the press and television correspondents began calling his talk "Solzhenitsyn's Harvard speech." Subsequent editorials, columns and letters-to-the-editor invariably mentioned the university as if the site of the address had given his words added authority. Perhaps even *he* felt that way. He had previously been asked to speak at hundreds of universities and civic organizations and had declined all of them. Knowing this, one of the reporters in Cambridge asked him why he had finally chosen to speak at Harvard.

Solzhenitsyn's response was direct and succinct. "Because Harvard is Harvard," he said.

One Harvard administrator explained, "The kids who come here want power. They want to stand out and be different. They want to get into the positions of leadership in which they will have an influence over people and events. And these new students don't question their motives in the use of power like your generation did. The tight economy has made them feel more vulnerable, and they want to be certain by the time they leave Harvard that they will have their place in the upper class. They're thankful to be here and they're determined to take advantage of every ounce of edge it can give them. These kids are like a new breed. They like structure and they don't like to leave anything to chance."

—Kate Wenner,
"How Harvard Fails America,"
*The Village Voice*

# CHAPTER I  The Undergraduate College

FIRST-YEAR STUDENTS and outside visitors are usually surprised and disappointed by their initial exposure to the Harvard University campus, which everyone calls "the Yard." Enclosed by an iron fence and the outside walls of the freshmen dormitories, the principal buildings seem dingy and obsolete. Most of them are starkly plain and rectangular, built with dark-red brick partially covered with ancient ivy, the narrow cramped windows emitting pale feeble light from fixtures installed probably before World War I.

But the initial disappointment is soon dissipated by the ultimately irresistible charm of even the dullest old buildings, especially as one inevitably imagines the ghosts of long-departed Harvardians ambling through the yard just before sunset— Cotton Mather, John Quincy Adams, Henry Thoreau, Oliver Wendell Holmes, T. S. Eliot, William James, or perhaps the ghost of Caleb Cheeshahteaumuck, the first Indian to get a bachelor's degree (in 1665). There were several other Indian students at Harvard during that early period, the charter of 1650 having specifically dedicated the college to "the advancement of

[13]

all good literature, arts, and sciences and the education of the English and Indian youth in knowledge and godlynes." Indeed, the second building on the college grounds was called the "Indian College," which incidentally housed the college press that printed John Eliot's translation of the Bible (1661-63) into the language of the natives, with an accompanying primer, catechism and grammar.

The first building was built in 1639, three years after the general court of the Colony appropriated £400 for "a schoale or colledge," which was to be located in "Newetowne." In memory of the English university where many (perhaps sixty or seventy) of the leading men of the Colony had been educated, the township was named Cambridge in 1638. In that same year an immigrant Puritan minister, John Harvard, bequeathed to the wilderness seminary a legacy of £780 (half his estate) and 260 books, with which the fledgling institution was formally organized and named in honor of its first benefactor. Quoting a passage from a book titled *New England's First Fruits,* the original founders carved their motto on the college gates: "After God had carried us safe to *New-England,* and wee had builded our houses, provided necessaries for our liveli-hood, rear'd convenient places for Gods worship and settled the Civil Government; one of the next things we longed for, and looked after was to advance *Learning* and perpetuate it to Posterity; dreading to leave an illiterate Ministry to the Churches, when our present Ministers shall lie in the Dust."

With such modest beginnings, Harvard College eventually became the richest and most powerful university in the world. Aside from producing several generations of eminent scholars in every field, it has provided the United States with six presidents —John Adams, John Quincy Adams, Rutherford B. Hayes, Theodore Roosevelt, Franklin D. Roosevelt and John F. Kennedy—and several distinguished justices of the Supreme Court, numerous cabinet officers, senators, congressmen, governors, business and financial leaders, scientists, lawyers, professors, writers, publishers, broadcasters, doctors; thousands of men and women in all professions, whose multiple influence in our lives is probably incalculable.

It is, of course, a continuing influence (from womb to tomb, from Sesame Street to the White House), usually imperceptible but occasionally clearly evident as one goes from one department of the university to another. That all-embracing influence became especially apparent when Franklin Delano Roosevelt was elected president of the United States. Indeed, it was during the New Deal that most Americans were first aware of the enormous power that has almost continuously flowed to and from the various branches of Harvard University. And if one hopes to understand the nature and scope of that power, perhaps one should begin with the most powerful and controversial man ever to graduate from the university.

From the very day he was born, January 30, 1882, it was a foregone conclusion that Franklin D. Roosevelt would attend both Groton and Harvard. His father, grandfather and great-grandfather had gone to Harvard, two of them also graduating from the law school. So had most of his collateral relatives. But the university he entered in the autumn of 1900 was different from the one his ancestors had attended—more flexible, less bound by tradition—and the person most responsible for the change was its president, Charles W. Eliot.

Prior to Eliot's presidency, the vital center of Harvard was the Yard, the fenced-in commune where nearly all the students and many of the unmarried faculty lived in dormitories interspersed among lecture halls, laboratories and classrooms. With such close personal and professional contact between teachers and students, their intellectual and social life had been interpenetrative and thus created a rare sense of communal unity. But when Eliot changed the university's order of priorities, he necessarily deprived the Yard of the money needed to repair and modernize its ancient dormitories, several of which had been built before the Revolution. In his view, improved student housing would come after he had acquired "the most brilliant faculty in America" and had developed a truly great library (only the Library of Congress and the Public Library of Boston, among all American libraries, had more volumes than Harvard in 1900). Teaching and research facilities for "a graduate school of the highest quality" would also have priority. Consequently, student living facilities within the Yard failed to keep pace with nineteenth-century standards of sanitation; so that long after shower baths and bathtubs, once luxuries, had become necessities of civilized life, there were very few bathtubs or showers in the dorms.

Ironically, this lack of sanitary facilities eventually led to an increased snobbishness among students, which Eliot may not have bargained for. Since the university was failing to supply adequate housing, private enterprise moved into the breach and began building luxurious private dormitories outside the Yard, mostly along Mount Auburn Street, which only the rich could afford. So the majority who remained in the Yard, in addition to their physical discomfort, suffered the psychological stigma of being "unfashionable." And when the new private dormitories increased the growth of elite private clubs, Eliot's critics accused him of erecting an aristocratic society on the ruins of the supposedly "democratic community" he had inherited. But this was a specious charge. In point of fact, Harvard's student society had always been among the most rank-conscious in America, reflecting the caste system of the Boston society whose leaders had historically dominated Harvard's affairs. In the mid-eighteenth century the college president personally listed students, when they enrolled, in order of their social rank or, to be precise, according "to the Dignity of the Familie whereto the students severally belonged"—a list that was printed in the college catalogue and that determined precedence in such matters as table seating and service, position in academic processionals and even recitation in class.

This practice was officially discontinued in the latter part of the century, not because it was undemocratic, but because too many parents harassed the president for not rating their sons high enough.

Nevertheless, long after the *official* list was terminated subsequent presidents maintained an unofficial unpublished roster. Though Eliot himself never used any kind of list, the super-elite clubs enforced the same strictures with harsh efficiency. They accomplished this through a unique and complicated procedure of selecting or rejecting members, a system that some biographers claim "would have a profound psychological effect" on Franklin Roosevelt. The initial sifting out of the "eligible few" took place at the beginning of the sophomore year, when the oldest and largest club, the Institute of 1770, chose one hundred students for membership. They were chosen in groups of ten each, the most eligible in the first group and the "barely eligible" in the last; and the local newspapers would publish the list of names in the precise order of election, providing Boston society with a list as determinative of social rank as any president's list had ever been.* Thereafter, the chosen hundred were admitted into smaller clubs, with Porcellian considered the elite of the elite. Next in rank were A.D., Alpha Delta Phi (the Fly), Zeta Psi (the Spee), Delphic (the Gas) and five lesser ones.**

Perhaps because his half-nephew (Taddy "Rosy" Roosevelt) married a dance-hall girl nicknamed "Dutch Sadie" by her customers, Franklin Roosevelt was not invited to join Porcellian. This supposedly was "the bitterest moment of his life up until then," in the words of one of his relatives; it gave him an "inferiority complex," in the opinion of the remarkable woman who later became his wife; and he learned from it (this also was her opinion) "something of how it feels to be among the despised and rejected, a helpless victim of injustice."

Most people might find it difficult to empathize with such

---

* This practice ceased a year after FDR graduated.
**Cleveland Amory, *The Proper Bostonians* (New York: 1947).

upper-class grief, especially when they learn that FDR was offered membership in Alpha Delta Phi (popularly known as the Fly Club), gladly accepted, and somehow managed to survive with some degree of happiness.

For contrast, one might consider the parallel experiences of Felix Frankfurter, who was born the same year as Roosevelt, 1882. The son of immigrant Jewish parents, he attended Public School 25 in the Hell's Kitchen area of Manhattan, subsequently went to City College by subway, then finally went to Harvard Law School on a full scholarship at the same time FDR was in Cambridge. This contrast is mentioned because one should constantly bear in mind that there were (and still are) two kinds of Harvard men: the proto-Harvard men who are born to wealth and influence, and the neo-Harvard men who have had to make it on their own through sheer ability, through superior intelligence and considerable personal ambition—men like Frankfurter, Kissinger, Corcoran, William Coleman, Ben Cohen, *et al.*, none of whom would have been eligible for Porcellian or any other elite club. Which is not to say that some of the "wellborn" Harvardians were not just as intelligent and personally ambitious as the poorer students.

There are, of course, many Harvard men who have achieved considerable success and or power without bothering to get an advanced degree in one of the graduate schools. Aside from the previously mentioned six presidents of the United States, there have been hundreds of presidential advisers, cabinet officers, congressmen, governors and eminent contemporary public figures such as McGeorge Bundy, Douglas Dillon, W. Averell Harriman, Arthur Schlesinger, Jr., and so on. Scores of financiers such as David Rockefeller and Winthrop Aldrich are from the college, although one must conclude that they would have been quite successful without a diploma from Harvard or any other college. Yet it is interesting to note that the higher echelons of Rockefeller's powerful Chase Manhattan Bank have quite a few executives who were schooled in Cambridge.

Perhaps more noticeable, because they are involved in highly publicized professions, are the numerous Harvard College graduates who have been extremely influential in the arts. Skimming through various generations, one can point to writers like Cotton Mather, Henry Thoreau, Ralph Waldo Emerson, Henry James and George Santayana, and the more contemporary J. P. Marquand, Norman Mailer, John Updike, and Robert Lowell, all of whom have exercised a profound influence on American literature. In this regard, it is interesting to note that the *Paris Review* was founded by three men who had been fellow editors on the Harvard *Lampoon*, George Plimpton, John P. C. Train and Karim Khan, the grandson and subsequent successor of the fabulously wealthy Aga Khan, whose Ismaili Moslem subjects periodically honored him with gifts of precious jewels equal to his enormous weight.

In the field of music, the college can boast of several graduates who have been pioneers in their respective orbits: Pete Seeger in folk music; Alan Jay Lerner in musical comedy; and Leonard Bernstein, whose eclectic talent encompasses Broadway musicals, quasi-religious memorial chorales, and classic symphonies. Lerner and Bernstein, who met in the Yard during the late '30s, were later members of the elite (and very Harvardian) inner circle that surrounded their classmate John F. Kennedy during his brief presidency.

Even in the realm of public schools, where Harvard men are seldom found (though many of them administer or teach in exclusive private academies), one can sense the influence of innovative educators such as Jonathan Kozol, whose *Death at an Early Age* caused a furor in educational enclaves throughout the nation. One of Kozol's college classmates, Herb Kohl, has also challenged the status quo with his equally controversial book, *Half the House.*

Thus, in almost any field of endeavor, one will find the alumni of Harvard (once again referring to the *college* rather than the various graduate schools) playing significant and often decisive roles—generally constructive, though occasionally negative in the eyes of certain people.

But such preeminence is not altogether surprising when one considers the historic advantages which have propelled Harvard into its present status. Ferdinand Lundberg, an astute analyst of power and wealth, puts it rather succinctly: "Sure it's number one—but you've got to remember that it was the only game in town for a long, long time. It kept drawing the best people because they had nowhere else to go—except Yale, which was much too religious in the early years. Consequently, since power attracts power, which attracts even more power, Harvard became the world's most influential educational institution, eventually eclipsing Oxford, just as the United States has eclipsed Great Britain. Thus, even against enormous competition from several very fine schools, it still draws more than its fair share of the best students and will continue to do so as long as it maintains its highly selective process in picking its entering students."

Before analyzing the university's legendary student-selection procedure, one might pause to consider what outsiders think about Harvard. In 1973 the Ford Foundation conducted a survey of 1,300 college academic deans, each of whom was asked to rank several leading universities with respect to five fields of study—law, medicine, business administration, economics and science. Harvard was ranked first in law, medicine and economics, second in business administration and third in science. Stanford, the University of California at Berkeley, MIT, Caltech, Yale and the University of Michigan were clustered at a second level, none of them achieving first rank in more than one field. If one were to assign 15 points for first place, 10 points for second, and 5 points for third, Harvard accumulated 60 points, with Stanford receiving 30 points and Yale and Berkeley each getting 20 points.

But in 1966, seven years before the Ford Foundation survey, the American Council on Education, having evaluated the graduate schools of 106 universities with respect to five disciplines—humanities, social sciences, physical sciences, biological sciences and engineering—concluded that the University of California at Berkeley had the "best-balanced distinguished university," with Harvard in second place. Yet on closer examination, Berkeley's supposedly superior ranking seemed slightly skewed. In four of the five fields, Harvard actually outranked Berkeley—but in the fifth field, engineering, Harvard scored a zero, for the very simple reason that it doesn't have a graduate school of engineering. As one critic observed, "It's rather difficult to win a pentathalon when you are competing in only four events."

If one is searching for a more quantitative measure of the relative merits of both universities, one might consider the following: among the high school seniors who applied to both Berkeley and Harvard in the 1967–68 academic year, Harvard rejected 122 applicants whom Berkeley accepted, whereas not a single student accepted by Harvard was rejected by Berkeley.

Since most high school seniors apply to more than one college, with the most outstanding applicants getting multiple acceptances, every college necessarily accepts more prospects than it actually expects. MIT, for example, generally assumes that about 60% of those accepted will eventually choose to come, and therefore sends 1,600 letters of acceptance for 900 freshman vacancies. Among the other Ivy League colleges, the "expectation rate" gradually escalates from Columbia (61%) to Brown (67%) to Yale (70%), and finally jumps to 87% for Harvard, which accepts about 1,375 applicants for a projected freshman class of 1,200. However, in 1969, when it correctly anticipated that Yale would seem especially attractive because of its new coeducational policy, Harvard covered its bets by sending out 1,400 letters of acceptance.

One would assume that each of these letters is the product of rather careful deliberation, but one would hardly expect a college to undertake the prodigious effort which Harvard does in selecting its freshman class. It is a year-round process, which becomes particularly frenetic between mid-February and early April, when the notification date arrives. During the preceding months each applicant's individual folder has become thicker and thicker, with most of the critical information reduced to computerized single lines on a data-printout sheet: class rank in high school, College Board scores, evaluations of extracurricular activities, teacher and principal recommendations, athletic achievements, Harvard-son status and other miscellaneous information which may tip the scales in the final reckoning.

From all these data, with special emphasis on academic achievements in high school, the Admissions Office assigns each candidate a Predicted Rank List number, which is a statistical prophecy of how well he will perform at Harvard. This somewhat esoteric projection was originally devised by Dean K. Whitla, director of the Office of Tests and associate director of the Admissions Office, who several years ago conducted a computerized study of 48,881 applicants for admission to forty-three colleges during a ten-year span. Whitla assigns the highest numerical rating of 1.4 to students who score 800 on all their college boards, and who also rank first in certain public high schools, with their other achievements receiving lesser statistical notice. The lowest rating is 7, and almost no one is ever admitted who rates 6 or 7. On the other hand, the college generally admits about 90% of the candidates whom Whitla assigns a PRL of 1.9 or better.

Nevertheless, there are certain applicants who gain admission in spite of a mediocre rating on the Predicted Rank List. Such students are selected because of some unusual talent, athletic skill or life experience. A Navajo Indian whose bilingual poetry has been published in the *New Mexico Quarterly* and who also plays Mozart on a handmade flute would be a prime candidate for next year's freshman class. So would the son of a migrant farmworker who has built his own three-dimensional chess set while majoring in math at three different high schools. Or a somewhat less exotic graduate of a Bronx high school who has composed complex choral music for the school choir and who has also played center for a championship basketball team. A fine example of such multiple skills can be found in Harvard's elusive high-scoring halfback for the 1975 football season, a coolly sophisticated black ghetto youngster who plays excellent jazz and classical music on the piano. He was majoring in music and hopes to be a "serious composer like Leonard Bernstein."

The admissions committee is always on the lookout for such human gems and quite frequently ranks them near the top of its preferential list. Not long ago it happily accepted a student from India who had twice won the national squash championship, thereby satisfying its penchant for foreign students and doubly satisfying the coach of the college squash team.

Yet it is still possible to gain acceptance on the strength of mere academic excellence. As McGeorge Bundy once said during his tenure as dean of the faculty of arts and sciences, "Harvard hasn't yet reached the point of refusing admission to a boy simply because he is intelligent." But if that were the sole criterion, the college could easily fill every vacancy in its entering class with "unadulterated brains." For example, in one recent year there were 105 applicants with the highest possible score—an 800—in the verbal exam of the College Board; 206 scored 800 in the math exam—yet only 40% of the first group and 41% of the second group were finally mailed letters of acceptance. Indeed, although only 1,375 candidates were finally admitted, more than 1,400 applicants scored an average of more than 740 on their College Board exams.

As one might expect, some of these high achievers are remarkably skilled in extracurricular matters. One youngster, who had perfect College Board scores on all exams, had also produced an animated film on the dissection of a frog, and another one had made a rather complex telescope.

On a lesser plane one will find a considerable number of students who vaguely (perhaps outrightly) resent the "monstrously bright." As one distraught sophomore recently expressed it, "All your life you've been at the top of the heap—in elementary school, in junior and senior high school, always number one in your class—and then you get to this place, where you are suddenly just an average guy."

Brilliant and imaginative students must perforce be stimulated and guided by a faculty which is equally or more intelligent, as well as mature and continuously provocative. Although certain prima donnas have occasionally shown a hint of disdain or impatience with respect to their undergraduate students, the college has usually managed to command a fair degree of tutorial competence from its distinguished scholars. Better paid than most professors and not too heavily burdened with coursework (four class hours per week is the average), quite a few professors have had time enough to accomplish the kind of original research that garners such recognition as the Nobel Prize, which has been awarded to at least thirty-eight past and present members of the Harvard University.

Among the most likely future recipients of the Nobel Prize are four of the university's most brilliant biochemists, Agiris Efstratiades, Fotis Kafatos, Thomas Maniatis and Allen Maxam, who recently have duplicated a mammalian gene, a unit of the DNA molecule that transmits a specific inherited trait; they have artificially created the gene that orders the production of hemoglobin—a blood component—in rabbits. Kafatos believes it is possible to make the entire hemoglobin, which could bring scientists closer to solving the mystery of life itself.

Unfortunately, some of these learned men are poor performers in the classroom, often mumbling to themselves or lapsing into long meditative silences, perhaps pondering an elusive nuance of a new theorem. In fact, many students prefer substitute lectures by lab assistants or young instructors angling for tenure. In any event, the undergraduates make a yearly appraisal of the teaching abilities of the faculty, which is published by the undergraduate student newspaper, the *Crimson;* and some of their comments about professors can be devastatingly caustic or humorously indifferent.

In addition to its regular curriculum, the college offers a freshman seminar program, with visiting scholars, artists and writers whose names are generally world-renowned. There are now more then forty special seminars, some of which are so popular and oversubscribed that many freshmen have complained that "you've got to compete in a rat race to get into one." In one recent year more than 140 Harvard and Radcliffe students vied for ten places in a seminar called "The Nature of Human Emotions." About 130 applied for twelve seats in "The Psychoanalytic View of Man," and 107 tried for fourteen places in "Computergraphics." The seminar on creative writing offered by Bernard Malamud drew ninety applications for ten seats; and the one on Latin American poetry by Octavio Paz has also been oversubscribed by a ratio of ten to one.

Aside from frequent journalistic references to specific activities at the college, there have been countless general or abstract references to Harvard in novels, nonfiction books, magazine articles, television newscasts and motion pictures, many of which allude to the university's reputation for excellence and/or power. Here, for example, are passages from recent best-selling novels by E.L. Doctorow and Saul Bellow, neither of whom studied in Cambridge.

> He's subtle, though. He's a subtle man, in a dirty way. Don't underrate him. And he's a rough infighter. But to become a professor without even a BA....it speaks for itself. His father was just a lobsterman. His mother took in washing. She did Kittredge's collars in Cambridge and she wangled library privileges for her son. He went down into the Harvard stacks a weakling and he came up a regular titan. Now he's a Wasp gentlemen and lords it over us. You and I have raised his status. He comes on with two Jews like a mogul and a prince....
>
> Saul Bellow, *Humboldt's Gift*

> Father attended Groton and then Harvard. He read German Philosophy. In the winter of his sophomore year his studies ended. His

father had made a fortune in the Civil War and had since used his time losing it in unwise speculations. It was now entirely gone. Coming into his majority, the orphan took the few dollars left to him and invested it in a small fireworks business owned by an Italian. Eventually he took it over, expanded its sales, bought out a flag manufacturing firm and became quite comfortable. He was proud of his life but never forgot that before going into business he had been to Harvard. He had heard William James lecture on the principles of Modern Psychology...."

                                                E.L. Doctorow, *Ragtime*

Once again the Harvard mystique is reinforced and expanded, the specific continuously converted into the general as the symbol becomes more and more deeply imbedded in the public mind.

There are, of course, several aspects to this mystique, one of which involves family tradition. As previously mentioned, there is a difference between the proto-Harvard man and the neo-Harvard man, with the former usually having at least an initial advantage. But occasionally the tables are turned, as in the following vignette from a yet-to-be-published manuscript:

Several spectators audibly hissed as the tall, lean, conservatively dressed Bostonian walked into the packed courtroom to testify in defense of Daniel Ellsberg. He was to tell the jury that Ellsburg had not violated national security when he released the Pentagon Papers, many of which the witness himself had written.

"What's that sonofabitch doing here?" muttered a bearded young man with a peace symbol on the sleeve of his dungaree jacket.

"He has come to do penance," said the middle-aged lawyer sitting next to him. "This is an act of contrition—by which he hopes to be forgiven by all his former colleagues at Harvard. But I'm afraid it won't be that easy. They'll still ostracize him from Cambridge because of his actions on Vietnam. Those people don't forgive easily. And it's so ironic, because he's the very essence of a Harvard man."

He was referring, of course, to McGeorge Bundy, the perpetually controversial ex-dean of Harvard College, who had become one of the most influential men in the administrations of

John F. Kennedy and Lyndon B. Johnson, and was presently serving as president of the immensely powerful Ford Foundation. While still at Harvard, Bundy had known Ellsberg, who was a junior fellow at the university; and they had both participated (at different levels, of course) in the preparation of the Pentagon report which had been ordered by Secretary of Defense Robert S. McNamara, also a graduate of Harvard. But the previously hawkish Ellsberg had suddenly become a dove on the issue of Vietnam and had become bitterly critical of Bundy, who had once been called "my favorite hawk" by Lyndon Johnson. Consequently, Ellsberg, the son of Jewish immigrants, had become an instant hero in the Cambridge intellectual community, while the very patrician McGeorge Bundy was suddenly *persona non grata*.

The Ellsberg–Bundy incident presents a classic distinction between the proto- and neo-Harvard man. And one can also draw a distinction between what we call "tandem grads" (those who get a degree from Harvard College and also from one of the university's graduate schools) and "solo grads," who get only one degree from either the college or one of the graduate schools. Obviously, a "tandem grad" would seem to be at the top of the totem pole, particularly if he is also a proto-Harvard man. There are, however, certain people who believe that you can't be a "real" Harvard man unless you have earned an undergraduate degree from the college. Indeed, if you are an outlander attending the law school or one of the other graduate schools, you can probably guess which of your classmates came from the college. They seem to be more sure of themselves—not in a snobbish way, but in an intellectually secure way, as if they have already weathered the most grueling academic obstacles against exceedingly tough competition. There may be a hint of snobbery in some of them, but it's that sense of solid confidence that is most noticeable.

Needless to say, many people resent Harvard men, and sometimes their resentment veers toward hatred, which often provokes harsh accusations: "They're a bunch of damned snobs.... They're always throwing their weight around.... They stick to each other like lousy leeches...."

Unfortunately, such judgments are often disturbingly accurate.

At almost forty-two, Josh Hillman was exactly where an ex-child prodigy should be: at the top of his profession and possessed of an unlimited future.

He had grown up on Fairfax Avenue, the heart of the Jewish ghetto of Los Angeles, an only child, the son of the rabbi of a small, shabby synagogue. By the age of two-and-a-half, he could read; by fourteen-and-a-half he had been granted a full scholarship at Harvard; at eighteen-and-a-half he had been graduated summa cum laude, and at twenty-one-and-a-half he had been graduated from Harvard Law School as an editor of the *Harvard Law Review*, an editorship that is no more eagerly sought or won than that of *The New York Times*.

—Judith Krantz,
*Scruples*

CHAPTER II  The Harvard Law School

UNDOUBTEDLY the most prestigious and notorious branch of the university, the Harvard Law School has had an incalculable influence in the legal, political and economic affairs of this nation. Harvard lawyers, a most incestuous group, dominate a lion's share of the most powerful law firms in every major city of this country. They occupy (and have always occupied) top-echelon positions in the federal government and in the judiciary, having long ago established an ever-expanding white-collar "mafia" that takes care of its own. Many non-Harvard lawyers are acutely aware of this power syndrome and deeply resent it, but very few are aware of the law school's influence *outside* the United States. There are, in fact, more than 1,600 lawyers in ninety-six countries who have studied in Cambridge, many of whom wield enormous power. (Saudi Arabia's minister of oil, Ahmed Zaki Yamani, graduated from the Harvard Law School in 1966.) Eighty-two Harvard lawyers practice in Tokyo, 104 in London, seventy-two in Paris, thirty-seven in Mexico City; and there are two in the remote capital of Chad.

Whenever a Harvard lawyer wishes to refer a case to a fellow

[31]

Harvardian in another state or country, he simply thumbs through the mammoth 1,490-page *Harvard Law School Alumni Directory*, which lists several thousand names and addresses conveniently classified as to state, country, year of graduation and current law firm or governmental position. Needless to say, this periodically revised directory has included the names of some of the most distinguished jurists and lawyers in American history: Oliver Wendell Holmes, Louis Brandeis, Felix Frankfurter, Learned Hand, Dean Acheson, Harold Stimson, David Lilienthal, Sam Ervin, Elliot Richardson, Archibald Cox and numerous others who have had a profound influence in all our lives.

The ubiquitous influence of the law school was often invisible in earlier years, but it became clearly evident when Roosevelt moved into the White House in 1932, after having served as Governor of New York. From the very beginning there was a constant flow of Harvard men into every level of government, and one of the principal conduits was Felix Frankfurter. Possessed of a towering intellect (he ranked first in his class at the law school for three successive years), the diminutive professor had made a most favorable impression on Roosevelt when they worked together on certain personnel problems for the War Department in 1917. It was Frankfurter's keen pragmatic sense of governmental power relations, his quick grasp of increasingly intricate bureaucratic problems, that set him several notches above most of his colleagues. Their casual friendship became more intimate as the years went by, Roosevelt periodically asking the professor's advice on certain administrative and quasi-political matters, particularly during his term as governor. Consequently, when he was elected president, "my good friend Felix" was among the first persons he called upon for in-depth counseling on all facets of government.

Eventually, Roosevelt asked Frankfurter to serve as solicitor general, promising him an appointment to the Supreme Court at the first available opportunity. But the offer was politely declined by the learned professor with gentle candor: "Well, I don't think it's a wise way of life to take a job I don't want because it may lead to another, which I'm not at all sure I'd want." But he nevertheless promised to think it over.

Shortly thereafter Frankfurter told the president that he had decided to stay at the law school, but would be happy to offer advice and recommend people for various government agencies. He was, in fact, an inveterate talent scout. For many years he had supplied his best students as law clerks for Justice Holmes, Justice Brandeis, Justice Cardoza and several judges on the U.S. Circuit Court of Appeals, such as Judge Learned Hand and Judge Julian Mack. He had also been recommending young graduates of the law school to the most prestigious firms on Wall Street and Washington—Sullivan & Cromwell; Root, Clark, Buckner & Howland; Cravath, Swain & Moore; Winthrop & Stimson; and several others.

Applying that same talent-spotting ability for Roosevelt's expanding New Deal bureaucracy during an eight-year span, he became what he himself called "the chief recruiting officer," further stating, "There was a good expansion of governmental activity and need for lawyers, and there was nothing more natural than that they should turn to the institution that turned out the best lawyers in largest number....and so it happened that there came to be a considerable percentage of Harvard Law School men on the legal staffs of numerous government agencies."

Many lawyers will dispute (and will certainly resent) Frankfurter's chauvinistic claim that Harvard produced the best lawyers, but no one can dispute that there were indeed a vast number of them on the legal and administrative staffs of every agency in Washington. Moreover, they kept multiplying in a geometric progression, each new recruit recruiting two or three other schoolmates, who would then recruit some of their classmates—or sons of classmates. One need only consider the radiating effect of Professor Frankfurter's personal recruitments from 1914 to 1939 (twenty-five years), several hundred men spreading out into the federal government, the judiciary, the largest law firms, and the faculties of other law schools—and each one of them constantly reaching back to Cambridge to fill more and more positions, year after year after year, until Frankfurter's original cadres had proliferated into a veritable invisible army of lawyers and administrators whose day-to-day decisions affected Americans everywhere.

Many of these men were identified as part of the so called "brain trust" formed by Raymond Moley, but newspaper columnists—especially those opposed to the New Deal—generally singled out Frankfurter as the shadow behind the throne, hinting at dark conspiracies hatched in the faraway recesses of Langdell Hall. Political pundits like Westbrook Pegler imagined "the professor and his disciples" engaged in all sorts of power plays behind the scenes—often assuming that all Harvard men were a homogeneous breed who listened to only one drummer, ignoring the fact that most of the law school alumni probably hated and feared Frankfurter as much as Pegler did. Certainly, Roosevelt had become anathema to most of the "selected few" who had been his associates in the elite "Institute of 1770."

Ironically, soon after Roosevelt appointed him to the Supreme Court, it was Justice Frankfurter who constantly bedeviled FDR's administration with a complete about-face in his attitude toward some of the legislation that had been drafted by some of his most esteemed Harvard protégés. Time after time, he would side with the conservative majority of the Supreme Court as it declared that this or that Roosevelt proposal was unconstitutional, while Justice Black (a presumed southern reactionary) would vote with the liberal minority. Some people mistakenly assume that it was Frankfurter's "sudden conservatism" that prompted the president to resort to his ill-conceived, ill-fated plan to "pack" the Supreme Court by requesting an enlargement of its membership, so that he might appoint some additional justices more amenable to his philosophy of government. But

Frankfurter was appointed in 1939, two years after the court-packing scheme.

Justice Frankfurter's loyal adherents have always argued that he had not changed, that he had remained loyal to his basic judicial principles—that it was Franklin Roosevelt who had insisted on changes beyond constitutional limits. But as Dean Roscoe Pound often said, "That is a value judgment."

Meanwhile, the federal bureaucracy absorbed hundreds of Harvard lawyers, who served at the highest levels in the administrations of Roosevelt, Truman, Eisenhower, Kennedy, Johnson and Nixon, many of them remaining in the capital to engage in private practice, often representing clients who had business with the government agencies they had worked for previously. Since the U.S. government produces an ever-increasing chaos of legal problems, the number of lawyers in and out of government has increased accordingly. As a matter of fact, a recent survey has revealed that on a per capita basis, Washington, D.C., has five times more lawyers than any other city in the nation.

Among the most prominent (perhaps "notorious" is more apt) figures in this powerful legal community is "Tommy the Cork" Corcoran, a legendary wheeler-dealer whom many Harvard men would gladly disown. In the words of one Capitol Hill observer, "He is a lawyer who does not practice law—although of course his firm is equipped to do conventional legal work. He is an insider who has said publicly that his utility to a client derives from his ability to find out things a few hours earlier than other people. He is a man who has dealt with the federal government for more than thirty years on public-policy issues, yet has left a minimal public trace. The back room, not the courtroom or hearing room, is Tommy Corcoran's haunt." A regular habitué of the halls of Congress, where he hobnobs with a diminishing number of old friends, he is one of the few surviving intimates of FDR, who nevertheless had no problem partying with conservative cohorts of Richard Nixon.

Indeed, his continuing contacts with the high and the mighty of both major parties have enabled Corcoran to accumulate such clients as Pan American World Airlines, which has paid him a regular retainer of $30,000 a year, although its "real legal work" is done by another firm. He also represents Tennessee Gas Transmission Company in its dealings with the Federal Power Commission; United Fruit Company, which relies on him to "keep in touch" with State Department officials in charge of certain Latin American countries; and El Paso Natural Gas Company, which has desired legislation exempting gas-pipeline companies from restrictive antitrust laws. All of these firms (and numerous others) pay him retainers that bear no relation to the usual so-much-per-hour basis generally used by most law firms, so that no one knows how much time Corcoran actually devotes to their problems. Nor do they know *what* he does or *how* he does it. In any event, he has no need for an appointments book, no time sheets to record hours allocated to specific clients and no record of telephone calls. "I move too fast to be able to keep a diary," he told one reporter. "We can't work on a time-sheet basis in my office for any purpose."

Occasionally, however, one of his clients gets a fugitive glimpse of the Corcoran *modus operandi*. Several years ago a tool-and-die manufacturer was threatened with default on a huge Pentagon contract, the Defense Department having discovered defective welding on a large quantity of metal barrels. Covington & Burling, the company's regular counsel, tried to resolve the matter through normal channels but apparently had no success whatever, since it was obviously a clear-cut case against their client. Finally, one of the law firm's senior partners advised the company to see Tom Corcoran, to whom C&B often referred its more "ticklish" matters.

The following morning, the company's principal officers met with Corcoran and spent about a half-hour explaining the details of their problem, after which he picked up his phone and asked his secretary to dial a number at the Pentagon.

"Would you like us to step outside?" one of the company officers discreetly asked.

"No, stay where you are," said Corcoran.

Then after a brief conversation with someone in the Defense Department, he hung up and smilingly informed them that their problem was solved. Needless to say, they were happily impressed and duly grateful. But when Covington & Burling subsequently relayed Corcoran's bill for $10,000, the company officers were outraged, even though the fee was much less than their potential loss if the contract had been canceled. "He made no pretense of doing anything other than that one phone call," one of them bitterly complained. "If only he had stalled around for a day or two. The impression was that he was putting the company on notice that he could get things done."

Such can-do arrogance inevitably worked in Corcoran's favor, and there were numerous clients willing to pay high fees for his "timely intercessions," among them an organization named China Defense Supplies, which represented Chiang Kai-shek in Washington. As general counsel for this so-called "China lobby," Corcoran was highly instrumental in obtaining close to $5 billion in military aid, which was channeled through CDS during World War II.

But there is another Harvard lawyer nicknamed "Tommy" who is even more powerful and influential than Corcoran. His full name is Herman Thomas Austern, and he is the most senior active partner in Washington's largest law firm, Covington & Burling. Though he is described in Joseph Goulden's *The Superlawyers* as "a nasty, rude little man who insults his clients and everybody else ... who walks into any agency with a meat cleaver in his briefcase and chops the hell out of any nincompoop who gets in his way," Austern is generally recognized as the number-one specialist in food-and-drug law. But in the eyes of Ralph Nader and other consumer advocates, Austern is the nation's number-one institutional evil, ardent defender of the cancer-producing cigarette manufacturers, skillful procrastinator for drug and food companies that often deceptively label their products, and, as Goulden's *The Superlawyers* would have him, "Manipulator of bar associations, backslapper of regulatory officials, and a one-man personification of what is bad about Washington lawyers."

Austern's opinion of Nader, as voiced in *The Superlawyers,* is equally unflattering and succinct: "Fuck him."

But whatever one may think of Tommy Austern's morals or tactics, no one can deny that he is a resourceful and highly intelligent lawyer with a complete mastery of the intricate codes that regulate thousands of companies producing everything from birth-control pills to peanut butter. His clientele during the past four decades has included some of the largest corporations in the world, and he has served them well. For example, when the producers of Geritol were threatened by the FDA, Austern single-handedly delayed the case for more than nine years, during which the company continued production without any governmental interference.

As general counsel for the National Canners Association, he led an early fight against proposed New Deal legislation for mandatory "quality labeling" of all processed food. Rexford Tugwell, then assistant secretary of agriculture, had proposed that all food products be labeled Grade A,B,C or D, so that consumers could base their purchase on quality rather than on brand name. Rallying the opposition with considerable skill and energy, Austern enabled the canners to defeat the Tugwell proposal and all subsequent legislative efforts of a similar nature. Consequently, according to a 1966 report of the President's Commission on Food Marketing, "the lack of quality labeling adds twenty percent to what the housewife pays for canned goods at the supermarket—the difference between what she pays for brand-name products and what she *could* pay for the same food marketed under a private nonbrand label." Needless to say, the added costs have amounted to billions of dollars.

Austern nevertheless refuses to accept credit (or blame) for the failure of Congress to pass legislation requiring quality labeling. "I'm simply a lawyer who from time to time has presented a client's argument on an issue," he says. "If so-called consumer advocates had a better case, and the support of the American people, Congress would listen to them." One may well wonder if he seriously believes that the average citizen understands the intricate legal reasons for the absence of quality labels on the canned goods they buy daily, particularly when they see and read an avalanche of cleverly worded industry complaints about "governmental interference with the American system of free enterprise."

While Austern's principal concern is the welfare of his corporate clients, there are numerous Harvard Law School graduates who espouse a far different philosophy. Many of them have organized "public interest" law firms, otherwise known as *pro bono publico*, and their most eminent guru is Ralph Nader, who got his Harvard diploma in 1958 and soon thereafter went to Washington to raise hell against the giant clients represented by lawyers such as Corcoran and Austern. He was soon joined by a continuing flow of young lawyers also trained in Cambridge, who were called "Nader's Raiders." Working together in massive research, they eventually produced a scathing denunciation of the auto industry in a report called *Unsafe at Any Speed,* which became an instant best seller in book stores throughout the country. It also led to several court actions which eventually cost the manufacturers of defective cars millions of dollars; General Motors was prompted to engage in a bumbling attempt to spy on Nader's personal life, which in turn led to a successful legal action by Nader that cost GM an additional several hundred thousand dollars.

Nader and his brilliant cohorts subsequently produced several other reports on various industries and simultaneously prosecuted successful court actions against some of the most powerful corporations in the world, meanwhile earning "subsistence salaries" more meager than those of secretaries and file clerks in conventional law firms. Commenting on the "revolution" he has fostered, Nader seems more tolerant about opposing counsel than one might expect: "I have never said the corporations shouldn't be entitled to retain their Lloyd Cutlers and their Clark Cliffords. The whole thrust of my argument is that there must be lawyers on both sides of a hearing room. The corporate lawyers must be constantly challenged and counterbalanced by the *pro bono* lawyers. That's what it's all about."

Several of the more successful *pro bono* advocates are also graduates of the Harvard Law School. William Dobrivir, who worked in Tommy Austern's law firm for eight years before quitting to help Robert F. Kennedy in his tragically terminated presidential campaign, has devoted his considerable talents to a case against savings and loan associations, claiming they have misappropriated interest received on escrow money. Joseph L. Rauh, Jr., perennial scourge of big business, applied enormous pressure on the Labor Department and the Senate Labor and Public Welfare Committee in their investigations of the murders of Joseph Yablonski and his wife and daughter, which led to the conviction of several leaders of the United Mine Workers of America, whom Yablonski had opposed within the union. Bruce Terris helped organize the Center for Law and Social Policy, but he eventually decided that the center's *pro bono* activities were being hampered by its financial angel, the Ford Foundation, which became "nervous" about the Tax Reform Act of 1969 drastically curtailing the use of foundation funds for political causes. Resenting the restrictions, Terris quit the center to practice law with Philip Elman, a fellow Harvard lawyer who describes himself as a "rascal fighter." Monroe Freedman, director of the Stern Community Law Firm, has had to fight disbarment proceedings because his organization placed ads in neighborhood newspapers and black radio stations announcing that his firm was willing to represent and counsel people who couldn't afford the services of conventional law firms.

Without a doubt, the largest and most prestigious "conventional" law firm in Washington is the aforementioned Covington & Burling. Indeed, it is probably the most powerful law firm in the country. Originally organized by three graduates of the Harvard Law School—Harry J. Covington, Edward P. Burling and George Rublee—C&B has been dominated by Harvard lawyers since its very beginning. Soon after it was formed on January 1, 1919, the firm was joined by Dean Acheson and was renamed Covington, Burling, Rublee, Acheson & Shorb. But after Acheson left the firm to become secretary of state, the senior partners decided not to add the name of each new partner, ultimately reducing it to Covington & Burlington. Most lawyers in Washington simply refer to it as "Covington" or "C&B."

At one time or another, C&B has represented most of the power elite of the U.S. commercial and industrial community. As one partner offhandedly told Joseph Goulden, the author of *The Superlawyers,* "We've done things for, I'd say, 20% of the companies on *Fortune's* list of the 500 top corporations." A less modest member of the firm frankly suggests that it's the *upper* 20% of that oft-mentioned list, which would include GM, AT&T, du Pont, CBS, American Airlines, U.S. Steel, RCA, Anaconda Copper, and so on. In its international practice, C&B frequently advises foreign governments and companies in routine matters, and occasionally serves as an arm of the U.S. State Department in "orchestrating activities of certain friendly allied governments so they do not conflict with Washington's foreign policy goals." Thus in 1946, when the Soviets were ignoring a formal treaty to withdraw from Iran after World War II had ended, C&B helped the Iranian ambassador draft his country's case for presentation to the United Nations Security Council. After months of haggling, during which the Soviets won a couple of minor points, they agreed to withdraw their troops, after which Iran was able to repudiate an oil-consortium agreement and also reestablish its authority over Azerbaijan. Commenting on his firm's behind-the-scenes maneuvering, a senior partner at Covington, John G. Laylin, subsequently said,

"This was the only time in the postwar period that the Soviets were bargained out of anything."

They have also advised numerous other nations, including Saudi Arabia, Greece, Turkey and Venezuela, relying on the expertise of Dean Acheson after he rejoined the firm in 1953, following his stint as secretary of state. So much has been written by and about Acheson that it seems unnecessary to elaborate on his towering intellect, his elegant, oft-forbidding demeanor, his occasional arrogance. He was undoubtedly the most powerful man in President Truman's cabinet and a dominant force in shaping an American foreign policy that was often a reflection of his own monumental ego.

But C&B's principal work is representing domestic clients doing business with federal agencies, to whom it offers a diversity of talent unmatched by any firm in the country. From a vast pool of 120 lawyers, the senior partners can choose specialists to handle any problem a company has, from patents on new medicines to export licenses for atomic reactors, from criminal violations of the Securities Acts to wage negotiations with trade unions—any kind of case one can imagine. Most of these specialists have been schooled at the Harvard Law School, and a few have gotten additional training in some governmental agency. Of the fifty-five partners in the firm, twenty-nine of the most influential are from Harvard. The next greatest number, nine, are from Yale; no other law school has supplied more than five partners.

The second-largest law firm in Washington, Arent, Fox, Kintner, Plotkin & Kahn, is also dominated by graduates of Harvard. Nearly half of its thirty-five senior partners studied their law in Cambridge, and its roster of ninety-plus lawyers offers an immense and varied expertise to a clientele composed of scores of multimillion-dollar corporations and individuals. It has also been called "the most powerful Jewish law firm" in the country, which brings to mind Felix Frankfurter's long-ago experience with the quintessentially WASP firm of Hornblower,

Byrne, Miller & Potter, which had never before hired a Jew. Shortly after he joined the office, one of the more friendly junior partners told him, "This would be a good time to change your name, Frankfurter. There's nothing the matter with it, but it's odd—sort of fun-making. Give yourself an appropriate name." Needless to say, young Frankfurter rejected the suggestion and soon thereafter left the firm.

For many years, he was the only Jewish professor on the Harvard Law School faculty—but time has wrought many changes. Now more than 50% of the faculty is Jewish; and the dean, Albert M. Sacks, is also Jewish.

Getting back to the preponderance of Harvard lawyers in the most prestigious New York law firms, it is interesting to note the following statistical data culled from the Martindale-Hubbell law directory for 1974:

Dewey, Ballantine, Bushby, Palmer & Wood:
 60% of the forty-eight senior partners are from Harvard Law School.
Sullivan & Cromwell:
 More than 50% of the fifty-seven senior partners are from Harvard Law School.
Davis, Polk & Wardell:
 About 50% of the fifty-two senior partners are from Harvard Law School.
Shearman & Sterling:
 About 50% of the sixty-eight senior partners are from Harvard Law School.
Cravath, Swain & Moore:
 More than 33% of the forty-seven senior partners are from Harvard Law School.
Milbank, Tweed, Hadley & McCloy:
 About 33% of the fifty-five senior partners are from Harvard Law School, with a considerable percentage from Yale and Columbia.

There are, of course, numerous smaller law firms in all major cities which are dominated or strongly influenced by extremely able Harvard lawyers, such as Joseph Flom, who has represented several huge companies in bitter proxy battles, and Milton "Micky" Rudin, personal counsel to Frank Sinatra, Liza Minnelli, Lucille Ball and several other entertainers and movie companies. Another Harvard lawyer, Robert Arum, was the brain behind Evel Knievel when he staged his multimillion-dollar aborted jump across the Snake River Canyon.

Less spectacular graduates confine themselves to the teaching of law. Indeed, 25% of the nation's law professors got their own legal education at Harvard. And the presidents of the two most prestigious universities also got their graduate degrees from Harvard Law School—Kingman Brewster, who until recently headed Yale; and Derek Bok, who was elevated from dean of the law school to the presidency of Harvard. The law school has also provided several justices to the U.S. Supreme Court, numerous judges for the federal and state courts and scores of politicians who have served in Congress, state houses and legislatures.

Someone has aptly remarked that Harvard Law School produces judges, professors, statesmen and lawyers for big business, and its curriculum does indeed reflect a deep concern for the vested interests of the power elite. The principal mandatory courses have always been Property, Contracts, Trusts, Corporations, Evidence, Agency and Administrative Procedures, all of which are taught for two full semesters. But only a single semester is devoted to *Criminal Law*, which for many years was taught by a sociologist. Consequently, Harvard has produced very few criminal trial lawyers. James St. Clair is a rare exception, but he mostly represents white-collar criminals, including a former president. Appraising the business-oriented courses he had to take, a black student once logically observed, "There isn't much in these courses that applies to my people. We don't own many corporations or utility companies."

The number of black students, still proportionately small, has increased considerably in the past few years; but they were less than 1% of the student body in the mid-1940s,* when William Coleman was an editor of the *Harvard Law Review.* Subsequently serving as secretary of transportation in the Ford cabinet, Coleman had been expected to be the second black lawyer to serve on the U.S. Supreme Court. But now that the Democrats are in power, that honor will probably go to Solicitor General Wade Hampton McCree, who graduated from the Harvard Law School in 1948.

For several decades (indeed, until fairly recently) the law school was primarily an elite, predominately WASP training ground for those who would serve what Ferdinand Lundberg called "the rich and the super-rich." And, not surprisingly, it has attracted the progeny of the already powerful (the sons of two secretaries of state, Acheson and Herter, sat in the same class in the late '40s), all of which inevitably has contributed to a pervasive mystique of power that seems to increase year by year. One other important factor contributes to this mystique: the high quality and resultant fame of its faculty, people like Roscoe Pound, Austin W. Scott, Edmund Morgan, Warren Seavy, Barton Leach, Paul Freund and Archibald Cox.

Occasionally these famous names provoke spasms of braggadocio from former students, as in the case of a rather tipsy Los Angeles lawyer who loudly boasted, "Listen, man, I learned my law from the giants—the goddamn guys who wrote the books," much to the annoyance of a far more successful (and far more sober) Stanford lawyer standing next to him.

Eventually, the Stanford man apparently decided that he could stand just so much. "You Harvard guys are the worst damned chauvinists I've ever known," he said, "You're worse than the goddamn Texans. And a helluva lot more incestuous."

"What d'you mean—incestuous?" asked the H man.

*The author, Enrique Hank Lopez, was the first Chicano to graduate from the Harvard Law School, and in fact for two decades thereafter, he was the only Chicano ever to attend the law school.

"That's obvious," said the other. "You stick together like a bunch of queers in a daisy chain."

Although his metaphor was slightly mixed, the Stanford man was certainly right diagnosing the Cambridge syndrome of "chauvinism aggravated by incest." Moreover, he probably suspected one of the root causes of that durable illness, particularly if he had seen the movie called *Paper Chase*, which gives a fair sample of the ambience around Langdell Hall.

As one immediately gathers from the opening scenes of that movie, first-year students are constantly reminded that they are supposedly "the pick of the crop," that only a few of the many who applied for admission were selected, and that they are damned well expected to meet the standards implicit in that rigorously selective process. If not, they will be among the 33% who will be "weeded out" at the end of the first year. With such dire warnings in mind, many a student has struggled through that initial year in a state of silent panic, fearing and hating his professors, often doubting his capacity to learn despite the Phi Beta Kappa key dangling from his key chain. Some very brilliant students have failed the somewhat medieval obstacle course—not for lack of intelligence but simply for lack of fortitude. And those who do survive are apt to develop an enduring *esprit de corps,* like survivors of a bitter military campaign or any other prolonged and miserable ordeal. As one of my classmates exultantly yelled when our first-year report cards came in the mail, "We made it, goddammit, we made it!"

Twenty years later, at a class reunion, that same man looked around the room at his now middle-aged colleagues and ruefully remarked, "Well, here we are again—all the guys who made it through that fuckin' first year."

He would now have to say "all the guys *and gals,*" since the law school has now broken the gender line. While all the other graduate schools at Harvard grudgingly allowed more and more women, the law school remained a bastion of machismo until the early '60s. Among the first female graduates was Elizabeth

Holtzman, the penetratingly intelligent congressperson who served on the House Judiciary Committee hearings on the impeachment of Richard Nixon.

Bitterly critical of Ms. Holtzman's relentless and courageous cross-examination of a Nixon defender, a White House aide sneeringly referred to her as "that noisy four-eyed biddy."

"Well, you'd better not take her too lightly," said a fellow aide. "She's from Harvard, you know."

Born 63 years ago in Kentucky's Bourbon County, Prichard was a plump, precocious child marked by a photographic memory, an early passion for politics and lightning speed through the schools. He was the top student of his high school class, and then at Princeton. At age 20 he entered Harvard Law School and again excelled. After his Supreme Court clerkship, he quickly took on important executive branch posts, and became a member of FDR's brain trust.

"Prich seemed to me from the start a man of dazzling brilliance," says his early and continuing friend, historian Arthur Schlesinger, Jr.

After Roosevelt's death Prichard returned to Kentucky, set up his own law firm and seemed destined for the governorship. But then, in 1948, he stuffed 254 ballots into boxes in Bourbon County. "In a stroke," Louisville Courier-Journal writer John Ed Pearce has noted, "brilliant future became nightmare."

—Neal R. Peirce,
*Washington Post* syndicate

# CHAPTER III  The Golden Passport

In a few days the world will be richer by 750 Masters of Business Administration from Harvard, a prospect that can be disappointing only to the 2,250 or so employers who tried hard to snag one this spring and failed.

—*The New York Times*
May 23, 1978

SUCH HYPERBOLE IS RATHER UNUSUAL for the circumspect *New York Times,* particularly when it is prefaced by a three-column headline that reads, "Harvard MBA: A Golden Passport." But the facts and figures would seem to justify a considerable degree of journalistic fervor. Indeed, the companies that managed to snag one of these highly sought-after graduates were paying an estimated average starting salary of $25,931—about $4,000 more than the average for the preceding year. And judging from the intensive competition among prospective employers, those starting salaries will continue to spiral at double the rate of inflation in other sectors of the nation's economy.

In the spring of 1978, the business school's twenty-six interview rooms were fully booked at half-hour intervals for forty days, with a substantial overflow channeled into hotel

[49]

suites in the Cambridge–Boston area. More than 12,000 interviews were conducted by representatives of the nation's largest businesses (a curious reversal of normal procedures, with the mountain coming to Mohammed) and 3,000 job offers were made, an average of four for each student. Anxious to make their bids at the earliest opportunity, hundreds of firms had already reserved interview space for next year's class, so that 60% of the available half-hour sessions were booked a year in advance.

This mad scramble for "B school" graduates is easily predictable when one considers the achievement records of former graduates, including the following "big wheels" of American industry, business and finance: C. Peter McColough, chairman and chief executive officer of Xerox; his predecessor, Joseph Wilson; William Sneath, president of Union Carbide; Stewart Cort, chairman and chief executive officer of Bethlehem Steel; Roy Ash, former head of Litton Industries and later director of the Office of Management and Budget for President Nixon; Llewellyn L. Callaway, Jr., former publisher of *Newsweek*; James E. Robinson, chairman of Indian Head Mills; Conrad Jones, president of the markets and products group of Booz, Allen & Hamilton; Walter Kissinger, president and chief executive officer of the Allen Group; Andrall Pearson, president of PepsiCo; Edward Carter, president of Broadway-Hale; U.S. Senator William Proxmire, financial watchdog of the Senate; Robert S. McNamara, president of the World Bank and ex-secretary of defense; Thorton Bradshaw, president of Atlantic Richfield. The list of successful graduates is endless. In fact, more than half of the school's 41,600 alumni are now top-notch decision-makers in the nation's largest business enterprises—"the people who really roll the snowballs," as the editor of the *Harvard Business Bulletin* recently put it.

In the words of one outside observer, "The Harvard Business School is not only the oldest, largest, most celebrated and prestigious graduate school of business in the United States; it is the rubric for 'the top' in the profession of business management." But aside from producing more presidents and board chairmen of major corporations, more key executives than any other business school in the country, its research programs have had a broad and continuous impact on business practices and educational concepts throughout the world.

Its influence in the oil-rich Middle East, for example, is almost incalculable. The huge and heavily financed Graduate School of Business and Management of Iran was virtually created by the Harvard Business School, which provided the shah's pet project with a full-scale curriculum and most of its faculty. With more than ample funding from the Iranian treasury, the symbiotic relationship between the two schools has been strengthened over the past few years, with a radiating effect throughout the Persian and Arab world. Thus, hundreds of students from Iran, Saudi Arabia, Kuwait, Oman and Persian Gulf emirates are learning how to manage their booming economies according to the sophisticated techniques developed on the faraway banks of the Charles River.

One should note, however, that Harvard's influence in the Middle East was immense even before the business school's academic invasion of Teheran. According to a report in *Fortune* several years ago, of the four most influential non-Arabs in the world's oil industry, three were graduates and/or former professors from the Harvard Business School who had subsequently become executives of this nation's largest oil companies. Nevertheless (as will be seen in a later chapter of this book), the collective influence of these American tycoons is overshadowed by the enormous power of a single Arab, Shiek Ahmed Zaki Yamani, the brilliant, soft-spoken minister of oil for Saudi Arabia, who attended the Harvard Law School in the middle '60s.

The oil industry is only one of the many industries whose top-level management is dominated by Harvard men. They also occupy key positions in the New York stock exchanges, major banks, publishing, manufacturing, merchandising, advertising, insurance, the higher echelons of federal and state governments and all other sectors of the American economy. And as executives of multinational corporations (IBM, Xerox, Union Carbide, ITT, Alcoa, ARAMCO, *ad infinitum*), they are a major force in the entire world economy.

Still, despite the phenomenal successes of its alumni and its ever-expanding institutional prestige, the Harvard Business School ranks very low in the academic pecking order of the Harvard community, almost as low as the bottom-level Harvard Graduate School of Education. At the elite, ultra-snobbish cocktail and dinner parties in Cambridge and its suburbs, one will seldom (if ever) encounter a professor from the B school— unless he happens to be a proto-Harvard man like George Cabot Lodge, whose name reminds one of the age-old description of upper-crust Boston, "where the Lowells talk to the Cabots, and the Cabots talk only to God"—and vice versa. Isolated both physically and ideologically from the rest of the university (it's on the *right* side of the river), the business school is disdainfully considered a glorified vocational school by most Harvard intellectuals, an attitude graphically reflected in the remarks of a Radcliffe College anthropology student: "I could never date one of those business students. What would we talk about—aside from the Dow Jones average or the latest issue of the *Reader's Digest?*"

Her sneering allusion to *Reader's Digest* no doubt refers to the limited curriculum of the B school, which is mainly concerned with the nuts and bolts of everyday business practice. Because of its narrow intellectual scope, the faculty offers only a master's degree in business administration (M.B.A.), while all other Harvard graduate schools confer doctoral degrees. Consequently, the business students may learn very little about such abstruse matters as Weber's vector analysis, J. R. Hicks' theory of value, Modigliani's envelope curve, or Leontief's input-output analysis —but they are extremely well versed on the practical aspects of cost-benefit ratios, stock options, cash flow, arbitrage, currency exchange and tax shelters. As one biz-ad student frankly explained, "We're not interested in fancy theories—we just want to make a lot of money, and we're working our ass off to learn how!"

They do, indeed, work hard—very hard—as anyone who has visited the B school will readily attest. One such visitor, Patricia Linden, very succinctly captured the beaverlike ambience in an article for *Esquire* magazine: "The air in the classrooms is so charged with electricity you can almost touch the vitality, the dynamism, the keenness to become involved. Senses are alert, ideas crackle, intellects eager to miss nothing and accomplish everything are on the *qui vive*. These are the achievers; the men and women who make the 66-year-old Harvard Graduate School of Business Administration different from and a league beyond any place else in the world. Here, in this enclave of mannerly Georgian buildings, tomorrow's executive elite is preparing to take charge. It has been said that America is run by this zestful entity, and in no small demonstrable measure the saying is true."

Occasionally (infrequently, to be sure), one of these ardent overachievers will sneak away from his studies for some boozy relaxation in a local bar. One self-styled "refugee from the salt mines" spent a long evening studiously imbibing eleven different kinds of highballs and cocktails (from Scotch on the rocks to a brandy Alexander), periodically informing the worried bartender that "I'm just keeping my options open. That's what my goddam professor always says—'Keep your options open'—and that's exactly what I'm doing."

Finally, after all the other customers had disappeared, the bartender gently told him, "I'm sorry to close your options, Mac, but it's way past my bedtime."

"That's okay, partner," said the student with a bleary wink. "I've got another tax shelter across the river."

From this bit of evidence, one might conclude that certain biz-ad students are never completely free from the academic grind, that they are obsessed by business jargon even in their most dogged attempts at relaxation. Indeed, this may be the syndrome of graduate students in any discipline. On the other hand, as a prominent psychologist recently declared, "Only obsessive behavior can guarantee professional success." If such is the case, the Harvard Business School provides an ideal setting for such behavior.

First, of all, it provides a hungering competitive atmosphere by generating at least 10,000 requests for application forms, from which only 750 applicants are chosen for the two-year M.B.A. course. And that period of intensive instruction may cost $50,000 when tuition, books, living expenses and two years of foregone income are taken into account. But the immediate financial sacrifice seems warranted by the quick returns after graduation. Most of the 1978 graduating class began new jobs at salaries $8,000 higher than what they had earned just before they entered Harvard in 1976. And a recent survey shows that students who graduated ten years earlier were making an average of $56,000 a year.

"But the money isn't everything," says a member of that particular class. "What really counts is *power*, the power to make decisions that have a real impact on your entire industry, the power to move people when and how you want to move them, and the power to screw some S.O.B. before he screws you."

Quite obviously, the will for power is one of the basic ingredients in big business, and the B school's admission process can detect that particular ingredient with unerring accuracy. At the very outset, "the ambitious, achievement-oriented, assertive self-starters" are required to spend at least forty hours filling out an application form that enables the dean of admissions "to shake out the real gold from the pyrite." The exhaustive seventeen-page investigatory form covers three categories: (1) *academic achievement* (grade-point averages, mathematical and verbal aptitude test results, and admission test scores); (2) *work experience* (judged on answers to several penetrating questions and on detailed recommendations from former employers); and

(3) *personal considerations* .(applicant's level of maturity, career direction, reasons for applying, what they hope to gain from the course, and what they hope to contribute to the program). Several full-time administrators preliminarily judge the applications, then channel their evaluations to Dean James Foley for the final selection process.

Although 80% of the applicants are ultimately rejected, the B school has a far-ranging recruitment program to assure demographic and socioeconomic diversity. With its reliance on the Socratic method of questioning, challenging and intense discussion, the faculty seeks a student body with varied backgrounds and work experiences, a mixture of race, gender and career interest—blue- and white-collar families, the progeny of mailmen, warehousemen, business tycoons, clergymen, politicians, butchers and bakers. This human mosaic is composed of graduates from more than 380 colleges; but most of them come from the Ivy League, the U.S. service academies and the Big Ten; and the majority are (not surprisingly) from the WASP middle and upper classes. The percentage of minority groups—blacks, Chicanos, Asian-Americans—has increased from almost zero to 9% in the past decade—still less than their percentage of the national population. The number of foreign students has increased to about 13%, and women students have increased from zero in 1962 to 10% in 1978.

For Sarah Slater, the twenty-six-year-old daughter of a New York publishing executive who graduated in 1978, the M.B.A. diploma was "my gilt-edged credential certifying that I'm a bona fide businesswoman—that I seriously intend to have a career." Her first exposure to the B school was through her fiancé, Robert Brauns (now her husband), who got his M.B.A. in 1977. "I thought it was somewhat awesome," she later recalled. "But I couldn't understand what they did here—and I don't think you ever can from the outside. They teach you a whole new way of thinking in the very first year, and that changes you for the rest of your life."

The "new way of thinking" is produced by the case method,

which was invented early in the school's history by professors who wanted their students to examine and analyze actual business problems and to evolve possible decisions for each problem. After considerable faculty fieldwork, the "cases" are presented in ten- to twenty-five-page descriptions, with difficult sets of circumstances taken from specific business organizations. One case may involve a confusing spectrum of problems in the medical-products industry—with new marketing techniques, revised federal regulations, reinvestment alternatives, possible plant expansion, wage negotiations on expiring contracts, etc. And most of the problems will be so complex that no single "right answer" can be found—a situation that can be extremely frustrating for students accustomed to doctrinaire education, in which the teacher or textbook offers "logical solutions."

More than twenty-five years ago, Professor Charles Gragg enunciated the philosophical premise of the case method: "The assumption that it is possible by a simple process of telling to pass on knowledge in a useful form is the great delusion of the ages. In every business situation there is always a reasonable possibility that the best answer has not yet been found—even by the teachers." Dean Lawrence Fouraker, whose enormous height and chairman-of-the-board manner seem to dominate any room he walks into, has more recently reflected on the school's educational approach: "In the case method of teaching, students have to analyze problems that have no solutions. So you have to have a mixture of backgrounds that can be brought to bear on each case. When you have a good mix, there will be at least three or four students out of a class of eighty who have a better personal knowledge of the subject than anyone else in that room, including the instructor. So you get a variety of perspectives that gives the others, who have not had that experience, greater analytic power."

Aside from its continuing influence on succeeding generations of Harvard students, the case method has had a profound impact on the teaching of business administration throughout the

United States and in several foreign countries. More than 41,500 cases have been developed by the B school faculty since 1911, and some 200 institutions purchase printed copies of the Harvard cases through the Intercollegiate Case Clearing House, for which they pay a cent and a half per page, slightly more than the cost of printing. "Quite obviously," says one former student, "the Harvard way of thinking has become a permanent fixture in the business world."

But there are some businessmen who would vehemently disagree with that apparently unanimous opinion, one of whom is the owner of a garment factory in Los Angeles. "My oldest son talked me into hiring this fancy Harvard man," he later recalled. "Like most of the people in our business, we've always had a cash-flow problem, and he figured this Mister Big Brain could help us. But right away he wants to change everything— my bookkeeping system, my assembly line, my purchase orders, my overtime work schedule. He even changed the toilets from one side of the factory to the other—which was his only good idea. But he kept asking me questions day and night—about this, about that, about everything you can possibly imagine—always with this fancy Harvard accent and this low voice I could barely hear, like he's afraid the Mafia's listening. After seventeen years building my own business, grossing maybe $17 million a year, I'm supposed to listen to this smartass punk whispering all these stupid questions in a noisy plant? Not on your life, mister, not on your sweet life. I finally got rid of him after three months, even though it cost me a bundle to buy up his lousy contract."

A less jaundiced view was expressed by his son: "Dad didn't give that poor guy a chance to prove himself. First of all, his accent was no more Harvard than Johnny Carson's. And he didn't whisper—his voice was perfectly normal—but he didn't realize that most of the people in our business won't pay you any attention unless you holler at them. But all of his questions—and there were a lot of them—were damned intelligent and right on target. I guess they bothered the old man because every one of those questions put a spotlight on his major weaknesses, his slipshod way of doing business. But even now, seven months later, Dad is making some of the changes that were suggested by the guy he fired. To tell you the truth, it was his Harvard diploma that worked against him. If he'd been from UCLA or some local college, the old man wouldn't have been so goddam defensive. He's just a natural Harvard-hater."

If one can judge from the results of an informal survey conducted in June 1978, there are numerous Harvard-haters (or at least "detractors") throughout the business community of this nation. In a random sample of corporate executives in California, Colorado and New York—sixty persons interviewed by phone —nearly 25% expressed negative feelings about the Harvard Business School and/or its graduates. But some of their remarks seem to reflect an outright prejudice against anything that bears the Harvard label:

"I wouldn't hire one of those fancy-pants guys for love or money."

"They're a bunch of smart-aleck snobs."

"For a medium-size business like mine, I don't need a Harvard man. They're trained for the biggies like IBM, Xerox, GM, ITT—the real biggies."

"I don't need a Harvard punk to tell me how to run my business."

"We couldn't afford one of those guys."

"I'm doing okay without Harvard."

"They ought to call it the School for Big Business—which leaves me out."

A brief survey of its seventy-year history amply supports the notions that the B school is indeed the creature of big business. Although a mere stepchild of the university in 1908, housed in a basement classroom in an unused building within the Harvard Yard, the nation's first graduate school of business administration very quickly acquired a host of extremely rich supporters. Increasingly generous funding came from the General Education

Board, a private organization established by John D. Rockefeller, Sr., and from several aristocratic Boston families with prominent surnames like Higginson, Ames, Sears, Morgan, Peabody and Kidder. Enormous donations also came from the president of the soon-to-become-infamous United Fruit, A.W. Preston, who very pragmatically gave the school millions of dollars for in-depth studies of the economic resources of Central and South America—the so-called banana republics.

More modest contributions have come from former students. As of 1978, an average of 13,000 alumni make individual annual gifts to the school's general fund. Corporate contributions are made through a prestigious organization called Associates of the Harvard Business School, whose membership includes more than 400 firms and foundations, an almost one-to-one replica of the top layers of the *Fortune* 500. In 1973, the associates were divided into three dues-paying divisions with yearly stipends of $10,000, $5,000, and $2,500, jointly yielding several million dollars for research and case histories. Aside from these continuing donations, the B school has received separate endowments for forty "chairs," high-salaried professorships, funded at $1 million for each chair. The Xerox Corporation, for example, has endowed a chair in memory of its late chairman of the board, Joseph Wilson; Jack and Robert Straus endowed a chair in memory of their father, later chairman of the R. H. Macy department-store chain; and the founder of Indian Head Mills, James E. Robinson, was similarly honored by former friends and associates.

But the largest contributions have been earmarked for the construction of buildings that bear the names of the donors or their heirs: Kresge Hall, which has dining rooms for faculty and students; Burden Hall, a spacious auditorium; Cumnock Hall, which houses classrooms and recreation facilities. One of the more sumptuous structures is Aldrich Hall, built in 1949 and named for the mother-in-law of John D. Rockefeller, Jr. As described by the aforementioned Patricia Linden, "Its brilliantly conceived classrooms are all on the inside wall of the building, across the corridor from the windowed bays. And each is actually an arena: windowless, air-conditioned, light and sound controlled. They are set up as amphitheatres, within which long curved tables rise tier on tier to enhance the interactive structure of class discussion. At the front of each room, focal point for each day's drama, backdrops of electronically-driven blackboards whisk up and down at the flick of a button and are wiped clean at the end of each day by a green-uniformed maid who never looks beyond her eraser."

It's like a prelude to corporate efficiency at the highest and most luxurious levels, suggestive of such names as Rockefeller, Morgan, Dupont, Aldrich, Ford, Lehman and Sears. And as one reviews the roster of prominent individuals and corporations closely associated with the B school, one can safely assume that its carefully selected students will be immune to any Marxist or Keynesian influences from other branches of the university— that they will remain loyal to the free-enterprise ethos of their alma mater. "After all," says one of the younger professors, "We're on the *right* side of the Charles River, and we're happy to be here."

The British journalist Henry Fairlie, in an article published in 1967, implied that the institute was nothing but a not-so-subtly concealed staging area for the Kennedy restoration. He lambasted Harvard for selling its academic birthright to the Kennedy family for a potful of money (a $10 million endowment from the Kennedy Library Corporation) and pointed to the first class of fellows Neustadt had chosen—largely drawn from middle-level federal officials and other liberals—as proof that Neustadt was presiding over a commune of future Bobby Kennedy-for-President strategists. It was an interesting argument, mooted by the course of history.

—Michael Ryan,
*Boston* magazine

# CHAPTER IV  The Graduate School of Government: The Kissinger Seminars—The Kennedy Axis —Faculty Warfare

AMONG THE MOST DISTINGUISHED (or notorious, depending on one's philosophic appraisal) luminaries of the much-publicized Harvard Graduate School of Government is Henry Kissinger, an almost classic example of the neo-Harvard man who managed to prosper exceedingly well without the benefit of ancestral ties to the university. But soon after receiving his undergraduate degree at Harvard and immersing himself in the academic politics of the graduate school, Kissinger became the protégé of a proto-Harvard man named William Yandell Elliott, a brilliant, well-connected eccentric who quite frequently lapsed into spells of pompous crankiness. A staunch conservative and cold warrior, he was a powerful figure in Cambridge, particularly because of his solid, longstanding contacts in Washington, where he frequently consulted with top officials in the departments of Defense and State. With close alliances to conservatives in Congress, the executive branch (whether Republican or Democrat) and Wall Street, Elliott moved in the kind of sociopolitical ambience which Kissinger found most amenable.

[63]

Some of his fellow graduate students had expected Kissinger to attach himself to Professor Carl Friedrich, the prestigious and highly respected political theorist of the university's government department. Indeed, Kissinger had originally chosen Friedrich as his mentor, but soon thereafter switched to Elliott, frankly informing Friedrich, "I am interested in the practical politics of international relations, and you are interested in philosophy and scholarship." Thus, it seemed more logical for him to gravitate toward the sometimes flamboyant cold warrior who liked to be called "Wild Bill" and who was often called "Mr. Missileman" because of his close contact with the military-industrial complex.

Considering his long-range ambitions, Kissinger had made a wise move. Elliott obtained scholarships for his new disciple and later put Kissinger in charge of the Harvard International Seminar, which was designed for upwardly mobile young foreigners who had been selected as probable future leaders of their respective countries, all of whom converged on Cambridge for a summer of exciting and informative bull sessions. Although some of the discussions were not profoundly intellectual, they nevertheless gave Kissinger a chance to make personal contacts that would later prove very useful. Among his students were Pierre Trudeau, future prime minister of Canada; Valery Giscard d'Estaing, future prime minister of France; Gerald Ford, future president of the United States; and, on a less elevated plane, Birendra Bir Bikram Shah Deva, future king of Nepal.

But as one critic subsequently observed, "The seminars were not nearly so high-minded as they seemed to be." In 1967 an investigative reporter revealed that the prestigious Harvard International Seminar was one of many cultural and academic projects funded by the CIA with generous sums of money obligingly laundered by the Rockefeller and other foundations. "It was all part of the good fight against communism, to which Elliott and a lot of intellectuals at Harvard (and other universities) were dedicated," said a Washington official. Kissinger, however, immediately denied any knowledge of CIA involvement in the seminar, and there was a note of panic in his reaction when the story first broke. "Oh, my God, this is terrible!" he anguished. "People are going to say I'm working for the CIA." His fears were well founded. Many of his colleagues sneeringly dismissed his claim of innocence, and some angrily accused him and Elliott of deviously besmirching the university's reputation. Not surprisingly, student reaction was vehement and vociferous, with many of the angrier ones demanding that both be dismissed from the faculty. But Elliott's deeply rooted tenure at Harvard was immune to such pressures; and, through him, Kissinger was also secure. Indeed, Kissinger had achieved his security in a step-by-step process that required patience and perseverance.

Like virtually every other graduate student, he had wanted to remain at Harvard after completing his doctoral studies, but his department seemed disinclined to grant him a professorship. Consequently, with the advice and help of Elliott, he decided to enhance his status by applying for the recently vacated position of managing editor of *Foreign Affairs,* the quarterly journal of the Council on Foreign Relations. Since the council was the acknowledged "hub" of the eastern establishment's foreign-policy buffs, it seemed to offer an ideal setting for the development of Kissinger's long-range ambitions. Thus, although turned down for the position he wanted, he readily agreed to the council's request that he direct a study panel on cold-war military strategy, the members of which were mostly lawyers and financiers from Wall Street and Washington.

"I am happy to accept your offer," Kissinger told the directors, "not only because it seems directed in the main line of my own thought, but also because the council seems to furnish a human environment I find attractive."

Among the attractions was the opportunity to meet the power brokers who have always exerted enormous influence on American foreign (and domestic) policy, no matter which of the major parties ruled in Washington. During his first year at the council, for example, he met and immediately attached himself to Nelson Rockefeller, with whom he served on a panel concerning military security which was held at Quantico, Virginia, under the financial sponsorship of Rockefeller himself. Favorably impressed with young Kissinger's tough, no-nonsense approach to the cold war, the New York governor hired him to direct a family-funded project on national security, which was obviously designed to provide material for Rockefeller's projected campaign for the presidency.

In a 1958 report released by the Rockefeller Brothers Foundation, Kissinger weighed the pros and cons of atomic warfare and finally concluded that "the willingness to engage in nuclear war when necessary is part of the price of our freedom." This view (and others in a similar vein) had been set forth in his book *Nuclear Weapons and Foreign Policy,* a product of his study for the Council on Foreign Relations, which also published the book. Much to the surprise of Kissinger and his council colleagues, it became a best seller, and its theretofore-unknown author was subsequently described as "one of the scarier figures of the military-industrial-academic complex"—which also included Herman Kahn.

Perhaps because of the success of his awesome book (or in spite of it), Harvard shortly thereafter invited Kissinger back to Cambridge as a professor with tenure. With a secure base of operations at the university and a ready access to the powerful Wall Street lawyers and financiers he had met through the council, Kissinger had finally joined the "select company of cold-war intellectuals" who regularly commuted between Cambridge and Washington. Nevertheless, unlike many of his Harvard colleagues, Kissinger was never invited into the inner circle of John F. Kennedy's much-publicized Camelot. At the suggestion of Arthur Schlesinger, Jr., he was asked to join the administration and stayed in Washington for a brief period. But he was gradually eased out by McGeorge Bundy, the classic proto-Harvard man, whose high Brahmin manners were apparently more acceptable to Kennedy, who was himself a neo-Harvard man who had acquired the style and manner of a proto-Harvardian while attending the elite Choate preparatory school before going on to Cambridge.

Like Kennedy and his brothers, Kissinger was also a neo-Harvard man, but he lacked their preppy credentials and a rich father. So he had to make it on his own—and a brief résumé of his career in Cambridge offers a fascinating example of how the university attracts people with a will-to-power and often opens the doors to the power they seek.

Having won a Harvard National Scholarship—one of two awarded in the state of New York—Kissinger came to Harvard in 1947 with a cocker spaniel, an armful of typewritten reports and a severe case of jitters. "I was completely unsure of myself," he admitted to an interviewer years later. "I had just gotten out of the army and I felt like an immigrant again."

As for the typewritten reports, one of his roommates at Claverly Hall assumed that they were relics of a course Kissinger had taught at the U.S. Command Intelligence School at an army post in Oberammergau, Germany. "It was a fantastic array of reports on all kinds of subjects relating to European history, and I assumed they were about international relations, because Henry already knew his course and goals when he arrived at Harvard."

His roommates (in Room 39 of the most dilapidated dormitory in the Yard) were Edward Hendel and Arthur Gilman, the three having been assigned to room together because they were all Jewish and Harvard was still making room assignments along ethnic lines. Gilman remembers Henry as more mature than other students, working harder and studying more, often way past midnight. "He had tremendous drive and discipline. He spent a lot of time thinking. He was absorbing everything."

But according to a biographical sketch written in 1974 by Ralph Blumenthal, "Not everyone perceived Henry's dedication as a virtue. 'He was secretive, very serious, and had no charm,' says one old grad, whom we'll call Bauman—a pseudonym, since he prefers anonymity. Bauman offers a rare view of Kissinger's psychic intensity: 'He sat in that overstuffed chair—the kind Harvard rooms were full of—studying from morning till night and biting his nails to the quick, till there was blood.' ... Dr. Kissinger still bites his fingernails. That has been a fact of life in Washington for five years now. That he bites them bloody, however, would lend another dimension to it."

In any event, the anti-Henry faction in the dorm apparently resented his straight A's and were not so secretly delighted when he got a mere B in logic. "He was already playing the part of the German scholar," said the pseudonymous Bauman. "He wore the same clothes all the time for two years, at least.... He wasn't trying to impress the Radcliffe girls.... He was a 'sublimator.' So while we were chasing girls, he was reading." Yet, despite his reticence about women in general, Bauman would egg him into an occasional boast about a sexual conquest during his army days in occupied Germany, which he would conceptualize in terms of power. "He told complicated stories about how he would get the women who wanted to ingratiate themselves to those in authority. He always talked in manipulative terms. He was the man with the gun, the jeep, the coffee, stockings, chocolate ... those were the important things."

Obviously, students like Bauman were supercritical of Kissinger and undoubtedly envied his intellectual attainments. As Blumenthal succinctly observed, that first year would be Kissinger's springboard, he hoped, into the protective orbit of Harvard's prestigious tutorial program. A faculty tutor provides coherent long-term guidance on a one-to-one basis, and not every student then was entitled to tutor. Top grades were required—and in the postwar crush, with Harvard's enrollment swollen nearly double (to 12,000), the competition was hot. But Kissinger's marks were so high that he was assigned a coveted "senior adviser tutor." He got the man who would eventually project him into the upper levels of power—Professor William Yandell Elliott, the high priest of the university's government department, whose impressive contacts have already been mentioned.

One should note that Professor Elliott was also a major influence in the intellectual development of another student who would eventually join the power elite—James Schlesinger, who entered Harvard in 1946, when he was just past the age of seventeen. (As a GI veteran, Kissinger was twenty-four years old when he enrolled in 1947 as a sophomore transfer student, so they were both members of the "class of 1950.") Both graduated *summa cum laude*, and both remained in Cambridge to pursue advanced degrees, eventually meeting for the first time when they served as "section men" for Professor Sam Beer's Social Sciences 2 course. Having closely observed them as they helped him teach historical and political theory to undergraduates, Beer admired both of them but detected a considerable difference in their intellectual orientation. "Schlesinger was an economist with an analytical mind," he subsequently told an interviewer. "Kissinger was a philosopher, a political philosopher. Schlesinger had a more static kind of mind, while Kissinger was interested in process, problem-solving, following the flow of history."

Their later attitudes on the SALT negotiations would seem to bear out Beer's analysis: As secretary of defense, Schlesinger was primarily concerned about the "bottom line," about the number of weapons each side would have; while Kissinger seemed more interested in keeping the talks going as a means of "institutionalizing détente."

Both men received their master's degrees the same year (1952), but Kissinger completed his doctorate in 1954, two years before Schlesinger. In his dissertation, *A World Restored: Castlereagh, Metternich, and the Problems of Peace, 1812–1822*, Kissinger characterized Metternich as "a Rococo figure, complex, finely carved, all surface, like an intricately cut prism [who used] methods of almost nonchalant manipulation that he had learned in his youth." Castlereagh, on the other hand, was pictured as a solid, ponderous, pragmatic man who prided himself on "plain dealing." One of his colleagues later remarked that Kissinger's descriptions could have applied to himself and Schlesinger.

Still keeping ahead of his rival, Kissinger also published a book before Schlesinger. The aforementioned *Nuclear Weapons and Foreign Policy* appeared in 1957 and made a strong argument for the use of tactical nuclear bombs: "Limited nuclear war represents our most effective strategy against nuclear powers or against a major power which is capable of substituting manpower for technology." About three years later, Schlesinger published *The Political Economy of National Security,* a much less spectacular book about the role of systems analysis in politics and defense strategy.

Both men were university professors by then—Kissinger at Harvard and Schlesinger at the University of Virginia. Curiously enough, although Schlesinger was generally considered the more conservative of the two, his students viewed him as a leftist, while Kissinger's students considered him a rightist. But in 1961, perhaps because of pressure from more liberal colleagues, Kissinger seemed to partially abandon his cold-warrior stance. In a new book titled *The Necessity of Choice,* he wrote, "Some years ago, this author advocated a nuclear strategy. It seemed then that the most effective deterrent to any substantial Communist aggression was the knowledge that the United States would employ nuclear weapons from the very outset.... However, several developments have caused a shift in this view.... "

Years later, when they were serving as secretary of state and secretary of defense, their respective views offered a puzzling contrast, which prompted a Washington correspondent to say, "Kissinger's testimony before Congress often seems torn from between the covers of his book, *The Necessity of Choice,* whereas Schlesinger's testimony often seems ripped from between the covers of Kissinger's earlier book, *Nuclear Weapons and Foreign Policy.*"

Hoping to find out what their old Harvard mentor thought

about his protégés' current policies, the same correspondent asked for an interview with W.Y. Elliott but was informed that the old warrior (then seventy-nine) was in poor health. Consequently, he spoke to Ward Elliott, his son, who is a professor at Claremont College in California. "My father huffs and puffs about Kissinger losing his bearings," the son told him. "My father is a ferocious hawk. He is skeptical of détente and emphasizes military preparedness. He is against rapprochement with China and Russia. He feels this great softening will work to our disadvantage." As for the Kissinger-Schlesinger power struggle, the son was sure that the old man "would be much more likely to associate himself with Schlesinger."

There were hundreds of other aspirants-to-power who were drawn to Cambridge by the Harvard mystique—by that special aura of excellence created by professors such as Elliott, Beer, Friedrich, Arthur Schlesinger, Sr., Samuel B. Morrison, *et al.*— and one of those aspirants was Zbigniew Brzezinski, also a contemporary of Henry Kissinger, who got his doctorate in 1953. Though a brilliant and dedicated student with high ambitions, Brzezinski apparently was unable to find a mentor influential enough to get him a position on the Harvard faculty. So he went on to Columbia University, where he distinguished himself as a professor of international affairs and also attached himself to the Council on Foreign Affairs. Now firmly based in the establishment, he served on the Trilateral Commission, where he became acquainted with the Governor of Georgia, Jimmy Carter, who subsequently summoned him to Washington as his director of the National Security Council.

An immigrant from war-torn Poland at the age of sixteen, whose accent is only slightly less pronounced than Kissinger's German accent, Brzezinski has advocated a hard line on Russia and has been supported by his fellow Harvardian, James Schlesinger, who now occupies the powerful post of secretary of the Department of Energy. Meanwhile, their old schoolmate Kissinger functions as a head of the loyal opposition who, in fact, generally supports the détente policies of Secretary of State Vance.

Commenting on this curious persistence (and ambiguity) of Harvard influence on foreign policy, an old Washingtonian smilingly said, "You will always find Harvard men on both sides of the fence and quite a few straddling it."

Among those who sided with the hard-liners was McGeorge Bundy, the quintessential proto-Harvard man who preceded Kissinger and Brzezinski as director of the National Security Council. Brilliant and self-confident, Bundy had moved through the upper echelons of the Cambridge community with the assured ease of a man whose maternal grandfather (Lawrence Lowell) had been president of Harvard and whose ancestral links to the university formed an unbroken chain to its very beginning. But as David Halberstam pointed out, "Despite his breeding and traditions he was not pompous and not a blue blood in style. If he did not rebel against that which produced him, he seemed not to take it too seriously, he did not rely on it...."

Still, his background was certainly not an impediment, and certain things happened to him that might not have happened to persons less well connected. In any event, he became a protégé of William Yandell Elliott several years before Kissinger appeared on the scene, and was considered a "spectacularly good" section man in the government courses he taught for freshman. His major undergraduate course was Government 180: "The U.S. in World Affairs" (subsequently taught by Kissinger), which earned Bundy high praise from students who were particularly impressed by his dramatic verve and imaginative analysis. In fact, he was so successful and popular that the government department requested his appointment as a full professor with tenure— even though he had not earned a graduate degree. But, as reported in Halberstam's *The Best and the Brightest,* the suggestion caused some hesitancy on the part of President James Bryant Conant, particularly after he heard that Bundy had never even taken any graduate or undergraduate courses in government.

"Is this true?" he asked.

"That's right," said the representative of the government department.

"Are you sure that's right?" asked Conant, obviously unable to believe his informant.

"I'm sure," the professor answered.

"Well," said Conant with a sigh, "all I can say is that it couldn't have happened in Chemistry."

Some years later, when he was dean of the college, Bundy himself defied traditional academic restrictions when he obtained tenured professorships for three very eminent scholars who had no degrees in their respective fields: Erik Erikson in psychiatry, David Riesman in social sciences, and Laurence Wylie in French civilization.

When Conant left Harvard in 1953 to become U.S. high commissioner to Germany, it was widely rumored that Bundy would replace him as president of the university, although he was merely thirty-four years old at the time. But as Bundy himself later told friends, "I wasn't even interviewed for the job, so I couldn't have been seriously considered." Nevertheless, he seemed to dominate the man who *was* chosen (Nathan M. Pusey) and continued to run the college with bureaucratic skill and an intellectual flair that occasionally annoyed some of his elders. "He was so good," said one of his colleagues, "that when he left I grieved for Harvard and grieved for the nation; for Harvard because he was the perfect dean, for the nation because I thought that very same arrogance and hubris might be very dangerous."

Bundy had left Cambridge to join the Kennedy administration, having previously met Senator John Kennedy through Arthur Schlesinger. As Halberstam later described it, the Kennedy–Bundy relationship seemed preordained: "They got on well from the start, both were quick and bright, both hating to be bored and to bore, for that was almost the worst offense a man could commit, to bore. Rationalists, both of them, one the old Boston Brahmin, the other the new Irish Brahmin, each

anxious to show the other that he was just a little different from
the knee-jerk reactions of both his background and his party.
Whereas a generation before, the gap between them might have
been far greater (the thought of Harvey Bundy getting along
easily with Joe Kennedy does not, to use their word, wash), now
they seemed to be free of the prejudice of the past. Indeed, the
achievement of a close relationship between his son and a
Lowell-Bundy was what it had been all about for Joe Kennedy.
If they had much in common, Jack Kennedy still had some
advantages; though he was a new kind of Harvard Brahmin he
was nonetheless a product of outsiders, he knew the difference
between theory and practice in the society, the little things about
America that the history books never tell.... "

With respect to foreign policy, both men were hard-liners and
shared a belief in limited military intervention as a means of
helping "friends of democracy," a rather loose term for any
faction that opposed communism—even though some of those
factions were reactionary and dictatorial. There is no need to
comment here on the Kennedy administration's ill-fated intervention in Vietnam, nor on the expansion of that intervention
during the Johnson presidency.

Since leaving Washington, Bundy has directed the Ford
Foundation and has personally promoted and heavily supported
a broad range of liberal causes and projects—and so his negative
wartime image has improved. But so deep and bitter are the
memories of the Vietnam war that many of his former Harvard
colleagues seriously doubt that he could be invited to rejoin the
faculty or serve as president of the university. They no doubt
recall the student and faculty uprising that occurred when
Columbia University tendered and then hastily withdrew an
offer of professorship to Henry Kissinger.

Thus it is highly unlikely that two of the most famous sons of
Harvard will ever come back to the Yard.

Outsiders often assume, erroneously, that the university's
department of government is the same as the much-publicized

Kennedy School of Government, and the confusion is understandable. The Kennedy school is actually an outgrowth of the Harvard Graduate School of Public Administration, which was established in 1937 with a $2 million grant from Lucius N. Littauer, a graduate of the college's class of 1878.

Determined to distinguish itself from comparable schools in other universities, the school of public administration emphasized the *policy* aspects of governmental administration, rather than the more traditional emphasis on *managerial* techniques. This emphasis on policy was a reflection of Harvard's long-standing disdain toward "vocational training"—always a pejorative phrase around Cambridge. Thus challenging its students to "think deeply and incisively about the substantive issues of public affairs," its faculty hoped to prepare them for public service, either elective or appointive, but mostly the latter. Consequently, the school became a center for research (often on an interdisciplinary basis) on matters relating to public policy. From the very beginning its faculty was mainly composed of professors from other branches of the university, particularly the departments of government and economics. There were also links to research in the social sciences that might be relevant to governmental policy.

But as the school's new dean recently observed, "This specialized approach to policy studies had costs as well as benefits. In particular, as the 1957 Herzog study of the School noted, the neglect of the managerial side of public service left its graduates unprepared for the administrative facts of life in their subsequent careers. 'Emphasizing the program aspect in an administrator's life as intensely as it has,' the report commented, 'the School has tended to treat managerial processes quite cavalierly.' More important, however, was the issue of the School's identity. In his report for 1973–74, President Bok stressed the difference between a graduate school of public management: 'The primary aim of a professional school will be to educate students for positions of leadership in elective or appointive offices, while a graduate school will take fewer students and prepare them for academic careers or for staff positions as sophisticated policy analysts.' Bok voiced his preference for a professional school—which was also Mr. Littauer's original intention."

Yet, despite its prior aversion to practical needs, the school trained many future distinguished public servants, several heads of federal bureaus, cabinet members, flag-rank military officers, members of the Federal Reserve Board, ambassadors, congressmen, mayors, governors and a prime minister. Nevertheless, the school failed to achieve an independent identity; it was still a sort of academic stepchild within the Harvard community, dependent on other departments for faculty and other resources.

Conscious of this anomalous situation, in 1966 the Harvard Corporation decided to change both the substance and the image of the school. First of all, it changed the name to the John F. Kennedy School of Government in honor of the late president, a Harvard graduate and member of the Board of Overseers. And in the same year it established the Institute of Politics as part of the school. Moreover, as it moved to "professionalize" its curricula, the newly named school seemed to attract progressively more qualified students. As the university's *Gazette* reported in 1977, "In terms of academic performance, recent experience, and promise, this is the most outstanding class to date: mathematics and verbal SAT scores average 750; and the average student will have worked for two years in the public sector before entering the school."

However much the Kennedy School of Government may have been improved, it is frequently overshadowed by its appendage, the Institute of Politics. Allmost every week the institute manages to attract speakers or "visiting fellows" whose names are well known to anyone who reads the daily newspapers or sees the evening television newscasts. But its drawing power is no surprise when one considers the power and prestige of the people who serve on the institute's senior advisory committee, which includes Senator Edward Kennedy, Douglas Dillon, Mrs. Jacqueline Onassis, Averell Harriman, Senator Henry Jackson, Robert S. McNamara, Vernon E. Jordan, Jr., Katherine Graham, Otis Chandler, Michael Forrestal, Senator John Sherman Cooper, Robert Lovett and George C. Lodge.

Among the more recent visiting fellows were Tom Wicker, Seymour Hersh, Eugene McCarthy, Bella Abzug, Ron Nesson and John Connally, all of whom spent at least two days lecturing to students on the inner workings of the U.S. government. But while they were at the institute, several other prominent public figures were guests of other branches of the university, prompting someone to say, "When there are too many stars, none of them shine."

Governor Connally's visit provoked an angry exchange between a Radcliffe girl and her Harvard boyfriend. "How can you possibly hang around a creep like Connally when you can go listen to Chomsky instead?" she asked in utter exasperation.

"Well, I'm one of Connally's escorts," he said. "So I've got to—"

"My God!" she interrupted. "You're really becoming a starfucker, Ron, you really are."

"Well, how about you and Gene McCarthy?" he retorted. "You hung around him like a goddam droopy groupie!"

"That was different," she said. "McCarthy has integrity at least."

"That was still star-fucking," he said. "So quit leaning on me about Connally. But I'll see you at the Chomsky lecture, anyway."

With its aura of Kennedy-family influence, the Institute of Politics will no doubt continue to attract more than its share of so-called stars; but there was one occasion when the combined mystiques of Harvard and the Kennedys were not enough to overcome a seemingly small obstacle. Just before his death President Kennedy had expressed the desire to have his official papers stored in a Kennedy Library that would be an integral part of Harvard University. Shortly after his assassination, Robert and Edward Kennedy and other members of the family began a very successful fund-raising campaign for a memorial library, and I.M. Pei was commissioned to execute the architectural plans. The site first proposed was across the Charles River, near the business school, but the planning committee later changed it to the MBTA subway yards adjacent to college dormitories and closer to Harvard Square. Aside from bureaucratic delays that seemed a nuisance to the Kennedys, the project progressed as desired—but when Pei first revealed his architectural design in the spring of 1973, an exceedingly bitter controversy broke out.

Architect Pei's plan called for an 85-foot-high glass pyramid as the focal structure of the library. Reacting in horror, the wealthy residents of Cambridge—particularly the old families of Brattle Street—declared the design was too monumental, that it would make the library an overcrowded tourist attraction.

One of the principal organizers of the opposition, Pebble Gifford, later recalled, "When Pei came in with those plans and just dumped them into our laps, it was the first time we realized we could not trust the Kennedys. We already knew that Harvard never did anything unless it suited their own interests, and we immediately assumed that the Kennedys and Harvard were working together....they're used to having their own way and having people jump when they snap their fingers. We weren't about to jump for anyone."

Soon thereafter the Kennedys scaled down their plans and even eliminated the glass pyramid. They also hired the C. E. Maguire Company of Waltham to conduct an environmental-impact study for a $186,000 fee, which resulted in a report of 600 pages that finally concluded that although nearly a million people a year would visit the museum portion of the library, "the impact on Harvard Square will be minimal."

The response to the study was immediate and negative. "I have rarely seen a more myopic document," said a Cambridge attorney. "It seems to ignore the fact that this is already a congested urban area. I guess the parable about the straw that broke the camel's back has been forgotten. The idea of bringing a million more people a year into the most crowded part of Cambridge and then say there will be a minimal impact is urban planning madness. The Kennedys have buried their heads in the clay of the Cambridge train yards." Such sentiments were echoed by a small but well-organized group of community opponents who made no secret of their loathing for Harvard and their suspicions that the Kennedys had doctored the impact study. At the same time, the Kennedys and their Harvard partisans viewed the neighborhood association as "total obstructionists" who could only think of how to prevent the building of the library and not how it could be made feasible.

In any event, the Kennedy family finally grew weary of the opposition and accepted an offer to build the memorial library at the Harbor campus of the University of Massachusetts. Commenting on the angry disappointment of the family, a Harvard official gave his off-the-record appraisal of the prolonged controversy: "The decision clearly came down to the gut level. It was a tough decision for the Kennedys. They feel close to Harvard. If you base their decision on sticking it to the opponents, it looks easy, but it wasn't that easy. Sure, the Kennedys were bloodied a bit. But they roughed up the opposition as well. And whether it's football or museums, the Kennedys don't like to lose.

"Jackie was very bitter—bitter toward Harvard and the community. She felt that the university never really showed interest in the library. That they were more concerned with Harvard's interests than the library's. Then she was snubbed by the community and kicked around a little bit, and she didn't like that. But then Jackie never really exhibited any understanding about what a university really is. But it's a tough vulgar fact that U Mass isn't Harvard. The huge loser in all this is the library itself. After a while, all the players will be gone, but the library will remain."

In the eyes of most observers, the only winner in the

controversy was the shrewd, politically adept president of the University of Massachusetts, Robert W. Wood, who moved into the impasse in Cambridge and persuaded the Kennedys that the library would have an ideal home at his campus. Alluding to the fact that Harvard's Derek Bok may not have been decisive enough, Wood later said: "When you are the president of a major university, you do not sit tight when you have a chance to win a major prize. Harvard expects to get everything they seek, and they do not come up empty too often. But in this case there were complications and Harvard did not go after the prize and they lost it. In running a university, someone has to make the hard decisions."

Obviously regretting Harvard's loss, a fretful sophomore inevitably speculated about the future. "I guess when Ted Kennedy leaves the White House in 1988 and tries to donate his presidential papers to Harvard, there's going to be another big squabble."

Speaking of presidential papers, Harvard also failed to acquire the memorabilia of its most illustrious alumnus, Franklin Delano Roosevelt. Yet, with or without such highly coveted historical documents, the university has managed to retain its considerable reputation as an ultimate authority on almost any question that may arise. For example, when a British journalist provoked a public furor by disputing the authenticity of Alex Haley's prize-winning bestseller, *Roots, The New York Times* immediately sought authoritative comments from several distinguished historians. In an article headlined "Some Historians Dismiss Charge of Factual Mistakes in *Roots*," the *Times* referred to four historians—three from Harvard, one from Yale—leaving the impression that they were the only historians whose opinions mattered. As for the authenticity of *Roots,* the following opinions were expressed:

"It's a work of fiction," Prof. Bernard Bailyn of Harvard said of the book. "And its importance is as a work of fiction and a very powerful one. I don't think its importance rests on whether or not such and such a

ship was in such and such a place. I don't give a damn if they don't find
the ship he names. It's a powerful book for other reasons altogether....

"This account is the author's perception of the meaning of slavery,
and the account is one of sensibility. I don't think it turns on details. It
turns on a state of mind, and there's no documentation of that."

Another Harvard professor, Robert W. Fogel, coauthor of *Time on
the Cross*, said: "I thought *Roots* was the best historical novel ever
written on slavery, and I say that not to demean it, because a first-rate
historical novel can frequently give you a better sense of historical
knowledge than carefully researched history."

However, Professor Fogel believed that the publisher and author
had erred in describing the book as a kind of history, but he
suggested that it would be wrong to diminish the book by
pointing out that there were many errors. "*Roots* was a good
novel by a man who had done more research than most authors
of historicals. And I never applied to it the standards I would
have if it had been written by C. Vann Woodward or Oscar
Handlin."

Professor Woodward, a Yale historian, could not be reached
for comment. But Professor Handlin, of Harvard, was reached
and was asked whether he agreed with his two colleagues.

"A fraud's a fraud," he replied.

Although admitting he had no detailed knowledge of the
alleged errors but noting that the book had been extensively
reviewed, he said: "The historians say, 'Well, the anthropology
must be correct,' and the anthropologists will say, 'Well, the
history must be correct.' But if you add them together there are a
lot of interesting elements which raise the question of how a
book like this became successful."

Bemused by Handlin's acerbic comments, one of his younger
colleagues remarked that "since Oscar has never written a book
even one-twentieth as successful as *Roots,* he naturally wonders
what makes a book successful. Perhaps he's too envious to admit
that *Roots* was successful because it was a damned good book and

because millions of readers realized that Haley was expressing a profound truth about the black experience."

Several weeks later Alex Haley was a guest speaker at Harvard and was wined and dined by the senior faculty—and warmly acclaimed by the usually jaded students.

It was a strange match in a way—the Harvard lawyer from New York and the southwestern pol who felt so ill at ease with northeastern liberals. But both men had prodigious appetites for work. Both shared an expansive view of what government ought to do—the kind of ambitious, aggressive approach embodied in the Great Society Johnson was articulating. And both had enormous confidence in their ability to manage affairs.

It turned out to be a natural-marriage. Califano says now that either Johnson or McNamara is the most intelligent person he's ever met. "I'm not sure which." The President and the Brooklyn Italian boy who came to be known as the assistant president spent hours together every day. Califano says that in his last two years in the White House, he ate dinner more often with Johnson than he did with his family.

—Lawrence Meyer,
*Washington Post*

# CHAPTER V The Medical School: Center of Controversy

THE NURSE SMILED as she handed the printed consent form to a young black mother in the maternity ward of a Boston hospital. "Just sign right here," she said, "and I'll fill in the date for you."

"What's it for?" asked the young mother, merely glancing at the heavy print.

"We run certain tests on all newborn babies," said the nurse. "Just checking to see if there're any problems that may need a follow-up study later on. And this consent form goes into the file. Just routine procedure."

"Well, I want the best for my baby," said the mother, smiling as she scribbled her name on the designated line without having read any portion of the consent form.

This seemingly innocuous incident, repeated again and again at the hospital, was the initial step in a genetic-screening process that would later cause a bitter controversy at the Harvard Medical School. With its emphasis on basic and innovative medical research for many decades, the school has often been the center of intellectual turmoil—but this particular project, directed

[85]

by Dr. Stanley Walzer, provoked a dispute that verged on violence.

In 1970 Dr. Walzer had been awarded a research grant by the National Institute of Mental Health's Center for the Studies of Crime and Delinquency. Officially entitled "Sex Chromosome Abnormality and Behavioral Variation," his proposal was listed in the NIMH research catalog as "a study of developing personalities of infants with chromosome abnormalities with the objective to gain further understanding about relationships between chromosomal aberration and behavioral variation.... Personality organization is to be studied—normal or deviant."

But the specific abnormality on which Walzer focused his attention was the "XYY chromosome pattern," for there had been considerable speculation that the extra Y (male) chromosome could possibly cause "aggressive criminal behavior." Along with several other well-known researchers, Walzer had apparently accepted the thesis that certain antisocial tendencies were literally mandated by this "criminal gene," a claim that was presumably buttressed by sensational news stories erroneously stating that Richard Speck, the murderer of eight Chicago nurses, had an XYY chromosome pattern.

In the first few years of the project, during which Walzer and his aides tested more than 15,000 children born at Boston Lying-In Hospital (an affiliate of the Harvard Medical School), his research received only minimal notice—but in 1974 it suddenly became a *cause célèbre* when it was attacked as useless but pernicious research by a group of medical scientists headed by one of Walzer's own colleagues at Harvard, Dr. Jon Beckwith. A highly respected professor of microbiology and molecular genetics, the thirty-eight-year-old Beckwith had led a team of researchers who had first isolated a gene in 1969, and thereafter had received the Eli Lilly Award for his studies on the function of genes in bacteria. With such credentials, Beckwith proved to be one of the most formidable critics of Walzer's project, particularly when he was joined by an equally distinguished biologist from MIT, Dr. Jonathan King, with whom he wrote an article entitled "The XYY Syndrome: A Dangerous Myth," published in the *New Scientist* on November 14, 1974.

Flatly asserting that there is no verifiable evidence that having an extra Y chromosome causes criminal or antisocial behavior, Beckwith and King strongly condemned Walzer for deliberately informing certain parents that their children were XYY types and should be carefully observed over the years for possible criminal tendencies:

> Clearly, by informing parents that their child has a chromosome abnormality or, even worse, telling them that he is XYY, Walzer is creating a serious likelihood of self-fulfilling prophecy. Parents who are made aware of the possibility that their child may develop the various types of behavior ascribed to XYY's may very well respond, not to the child's true behavior, but to their fears of what he may become. There is ample evidence that this sort of attitude toward the child may engender the very behavior they fear, or create other unpredictable behavior problems. So, how are the results of this study to be meaningful if the psychiatrist's intervention may be creating more problems for the child than would have occurred if they had been left alone? This experiment simply has no control, no standard of comparison by which to account for the very real effects of self-fulfilling prophecy. The only control group imaginable would be to select parents of children with no chromosome abnormalities and to then falsely tell them the same information that was told to parents of XYY children. Only with such a group could a control for such effects as self-fulfilling prophecy be obtained. But telling parents of normal children that their kids are chromosomally abnormal is clearly immoral. There can simply be no control for this experiment. And, there are just some bad experiments that can't and shouldn't be conducted.

Admitting in an interview in the *Real Paper* to local reporters that his research methodology was vulnerable in certain respects, Walzer nevertheless denied most of the charges leveled against him: "Of course, as my attackers say, mine is not an ideal or perfect experiment. This is the first prospective study of three genetic populations of children. We're looking for specific behavioral variations or non-variations in their development. *And just because it's true that we can't have all the elegance of a perfectly controlled experiment here, is that any reason for my attackers to say that we can't have any controls? . . . .* [Italics author's.] Sure, a lot of the issues raised about informed consent and the parental consent form we used were valid criticisms. But all that stuff about self-fulfilling prophecy is just hazy nonsense. It's practically a religion—the way they wave around all the self-fulfilling prophecy shit. Do you know what the dean of the Medical School said about all this? He said, 'As long as I'm the dean, the newspapers will not determine the policies of this school.'"

The newspapers to which he referred included the Harvard *Crimson* and the local underground press, all of whom backed the critical stance of the recently organized group known as Science for People, which had expressed serious misgivings about "the politics of genetic engineering." The SFP was especially concerned about the "Harvard imprimatur" that would give unwarranted status to Walzer's research.

"The worst aspect of all this XYY crap," complained one critic, "is that Walzer is conducting his experiment at the Harvard Medical School—so that most people, including a lot of government officials, are bound to assume that his half-baked theories are the ultimate truth straight from the holy citadel itself. In other words, he's got that old Harvard mystique working for him, and there isn't much we can do about it except to bitch and fume."

But Beckwith and King, both members of Science for People, were not content merely to bitch and fume. In a formal petition to the medical school, they requested an immediate cancellation of the project and further asked that the school disavow any explicit or implicit support of Walzer's findings. Shortly thereafter, the school's standing Committee on Medical Research convened a hearing from which the press and general public were deliberately excluded. Most of the discussion at the closed hearing concerned the adequacy of Walzer's parental-consent procedure and the issue of telling the parents of their child's chromosome abnormality in the event that any XYY karotype was discovered. As principal investigator of the study, Walzer concentrated on the latter point and particularly stressed "the great care which we take in breaking the news to the parents if their child has this chromosome," cautiously advising them that their child might be "a little more vulnerable to life's stresses and strains." Nevertheless, he argued that the parents must be told the truth and that any deception could only complicate matters later on, and might in effect deprive the child and parents of psychiatric assistance they would quite likely be needing. He also stated that 50% of the XYY children in his study were already showing antisocial behavioral characteristics.

Responding to Walzer's assertions, his opponents reiterated their contention that informing the parents of the XYY karotype clearly compromised the validity of such conclusions from the very start—that there was no way of determining whether the extra Y chromosome or the parents' knowledge of it was giving rise to behavioral problems. Furthermore, they contended that there was no evidence that psychiatric intervention would do any good in such cases. Consequently, they were not arguing for a different experimental design, but were simply asking that the study be canceled.

After several weeks of internal debate, the Harvard Committee on Human Studies decided to approve the continuation of Dr. Walzer's project and announced its decision on January 22, 1975. During that interim hundreds of students and community activists joined the campaign against the XYY experiment, and their tactics ranged from calm academic discourse to actual violence.

One irate student had filled a plastic bag with cow blood and vowed to paint a bloody swastika on Walzer's home, but one of his friends convinced him that it would be an ambiguous and

confusing act. "Like, man, I know you're trying to say that
Walzer is a real fascist," he said. "But people might get the
impression that *you* are the fascist when you paint that swastika.
So you'll just be wasting all that oozy blood, man."

Though probably unaware of this aborted scheme, Walzer
was keenly aware of the violent opposition he had aroused, and
he expressed his concern to a local reporter: "My own son—do
you understand—my own son is asking me if I'm going to jail!
And all these threatening calls—*twenty of them.* Telling me I'm
a fascist pig. I have no shame about what I've done. I've never
done anything unethical or immoral. But this has been a hor-
rifying period of my life. And believe me, whatever the outcome, the damage has already been done."

With the eventual support of the special committee, the
embattled child psychiatrist felt vindicated, and he was further
heartened when fellow professors from other branches of the
university backed him on the grounds of academic freedom. And
it was Walzer's reconfirmed access to the Harvard label—the
apparent stamp of approval by the nation's most prestigious
medical school—that distressed his unyielding critics. They
realized that the project had been conducted in the wake of the
federal government's increasing interest in a very specific type of
research. Not yet recovered from the social turmoil of the '60s—
the "decade of violence," of ghetto riots and campus unheavals—
congressmen and senators had been desperately searching for
ways of reassuring their constituents that "things would soon be
under control." Consequently, they were more than willing to
fund medical researchers who might find specific *biological
explanations* for the violence that had erupted. And they were
particularly fascinated by studies in psychosurgery based on the
premise that violence was merely a symptom of brain dysfunc-
tion—or projects that might localize antisocial behavior in certain
genes. Thus, in the eyes of Walzer's critics, his kind of research
would distract the congressman's attention from programs aimed
at exploring (and ameliorating) the social, political and economic
causes of violence.

Beckwith had already noted that "Bently Glass, the former president of the American Association for the Advancement of Science, looks forward to the day when 'a combination of amniocentesis and abortion will rid us of...sex deviants such as the XYY type' (*Science*, Vol. 171, p. 23)." And he had also alluded to the case of a mother opting for abortion after learning that her fetus was XYY and hearing from the doctor "what little was known of the prognosis at the time...(*Science*, Vol. 179, p. 139)."

As for Harvard's continuing involvement in the controversy over "genetic engineering," one might reflect on the rhetorical inquiry by Arthur Jensen in his 1969 article in the *Harvard Educational Review*: "Is there a danger that current welfare policies, unaided by eugenic foresight, could lead to the genetic enslavement of a substantial segment of our population?" Reflect also on the statements of Harvard professor Richard Herrnstein in an interview published in the *Crimson*. Having recommended the gathering of IQ information as part of the U.S. census, Herrnstein said it could be used to "observe dysgenic or eugenic trends in American society." When asked what such information could serve, he replied: "If at some time in the future we decide that our population is getting too large, and we need to limit it, we could use census information on IQ to decide how to limit it."

Since IQ tests used to measure intelligence are considered by many psychologists to be culturally biased against blacks and other minorities, Beckwith feels that Jensen's and Herrnstein's theories encourage racial and class prejudice. "Teachers can now justify their biases toward black or other minority-group students. Social workers can now understand why the socially disadvantaged do not seem to be able to help themselves. And congressmen can now easily explain why compensatory education programs are doomed to failure, and are thus unworthy of funding."

And, presumably, they can all point to Harvard as a prime source for their beliefs on such matters.

But, quite obviously, the university cannot be held responsible for the individual views of each one of its professors. Given the wide disparity in the intellectual and philosophical inclinations of its large and egocentric (some might say egomaniacal) faculty, it would be impossible for Harvard to say that any one person speaks for the university. Like any other seat of learning, it should and does encourage an almost fierce competition of ideas within and between its various branches, and the medical school is no exception. In fact, some longtime observers consider it the most competitive branch of the university. Students and faculty alike seem to be engaged in a perpetual struggle for primacy, like crabs in a barrel scrambling over each other to reach the top, all of which inevitably results in the most jaundiced cynicism.

Take, for example, the cool response of a third-year student when he was told that a classmate had sneakily sabotaged another student's lab experiment by carefully urinating into several test tubes half-filled with various blood samples: "That's not unusual around here. But he'll learn to be more subtle later on, especially after he's observed some of our professors. I'm told that some of their sabotage—most of it on an esoteric abstract level—is so intricately subtle that only the most perceptive victim will realize that he's been pissed on."

Yet with all its negative aspects, such intense every-man-for-himself competition may be an unavoidable by-product of academic freedom. One frequently hears or reads about the notorious ego involvement of college professors, which is no doubt intensified by the fact that they earn far less than doctors and lawyers and must therefore seek other psychic benefits to offset that economic imbalance. Among the most coveted benefits is tenure at a prestigious university like Harvard, which may still leave a psychic gap for those who fail to reach the upper echelons of its caste-conscious faculty, wherein Professor Y secretly hungers for an invitation to Professor X's more sumptuous table...and would dearly wish to poison the food on that table if not invited. And hovering on the outer margins of the envied inner circle are hundreds of professors at lesser local universities, all Ph.D. graduates of Harvard, who have accepted teaching positions close to Cambridge in the vain hope that they will suddenly be summoned back to the Yard.

Meanwhile, within the university itself there are continuing internecine battles with various departments and between the separate schools, with a pecking order that places the medical school near the top. To the rank outsider, "Harvard" is probably an all-inclusive label, but to the insider there is marked distinction between the Harvard Medical School and, say, the Harvard Graduate School of Education. And it is within this context that one must view the XYY controversy, for it was a bitter dispute between highly regarded professors in the nation's most reputable school of medicine, with consequences that may heavily influence public policy in the field of race relations and welfare legislation at all levels.

More recently, the medical school has been the center of another controversy that has divided the scientific community and has aroused doomsday fears about tampering with nature— also raising the possibility of unprecedented federal and local controls on basic scientific research. The specific focus of this momentous dispute is a rod-shaped creature less than one ten-thousandth of an inch long, a bacterium known to scientists as *Escherichia coli (E. coli, for short)*, named for its discoverer, German pediatrician Theodor Escherich, who isolated it from human feces in 1885.

In several laboratories across the country, microbiologists have been combining segments of *E. coli's* DNA with the DNA of animals, plants and other bacteria, hoping to create new forms of life different from any now existing on earth.

The most publicized experiments have been conducted in joint projects at Harvard and MIT, where proponents of research in DNA—the master molecule of life—confidently predict that it can lead to new ways of understanding and perhaps curing cancer and such inherited diseases as hemophilia, sickle-cell

anemia, and Tay-Sachs disease. They also anticipate the discovery of new inexpensive vaccines, cheaper and more effective
fertilizers, and a greater understanding of the genetic structures
of plants, animals and human beings.

But the opponents of such research, while admitting its
potential benefits, are equally convinced that the inherent
dangers are almost beyond reckoning. Some scientists fear that
one of the newly created bacteria might escape from the lab and
find its way into a human intestine, multiplying and causing new
and baffling diseases more deadly than cancer. Others are
reluctant to tinker with natural evolutionary forces. In the
opinion of Caltech's Robert Sinsheimer, "Biologists have become, without wanting it, the custodians of great and terrible
power. It is idle to pretend otherwise."

Perhaps because they are graduates of Harvard and therefore
keenly aware of any unusual developments around Cambridge,
three very prominent officials expressed considerable concern
about the DNA experiments at Harvard and MIT, as well as
other labs. Senator Edward Kennedy, chairman of the Senate
subcommittee on health, held a special hearing on the potential
dangers of such experiments; and all the major news media
broadcasted and printed lengthy accounts of some rather
frightening testimony. Among the principal witnesses was
Joseph Califano, secretary of health, education and welfare, who
unequivocally asked Congress to impose strict federal regulations on recombinant DNA research, stating that "it is a scientific
tool of enormous potential" but warning about possible—
though unknown—hazards. Massachusetts governor Michael
Dukakis, whose constituents were understandably worried
about the genetic-engineering furor in Cambridge, also asserted
that the public had a right to regulate the projected research:
"Genetic manipulation to create new forms of life places
biologists at a threshold similar to that which physicists reached
when they first split the atom. I think it is fair to say that the
genie is out of the bottle."

Not surprisingly, the furor reached its most feverish pitch in Cambridge itself, where Mayor Alfred E. Vellucci immediately summoned the City Council to hold public hearings to determine whether it would withhold the building permit for a new DNA research laboratory. "We want to be damned sure," he said, "that our people won't be affected by anything that could crawl out of that laboratory. It is my responsibility to investigate the danger of infections to human beings. They may come up with a disease that can't be cured—even a monster. Is this the answer to Dr. Frankenstein's dream?"

In a similar mood of apprehension, three young mothers joined a protest parade outside the crowded hearing rooms, pushing strollers with one-year-old children and displaying signs that said, "Don't Spread Harvard Germs on Our Babies!"

Just behind them marched a bearded student with a large poster lettered with bold red paint: "Harvard's Brave New World Is Full of Feces!" When asked by a blue-collared laborer what "feces" meant, he said, "Shit, man, just plain shit. That's where *E. coli* comes from."

"Then why don't you say it?" asked the laborer. "Why do you need a fancy Harvard word for something as plain as shit?"

"You're right, man!" exclaimed the student. "You're right as hell. I'll change it right now."

And the crowd cheered as he made the suggested correction with a lipstick borrowed from a pretty nurse, whose protest sign said, "No More Monsters from Harvard!"

But, true to form, the toughest criticisms came from Harvard itself, from faculty colleagues of the DNA research directors. The most vociferous critic (certainly the most prestigious) was Professor George Wald, the 1967 Nobel Prize winner for biology, who told newsmen that "instead of trying to find the roots of cancer through genetic research, society can fight the disease more effectively by taking carcinogens out of the environment." Wald and other opponents of the project infuriated such proponents as James Watson, who had shared a Nobel

Prize with Francis Crick for determining the double-helix structure of the DNA molecule. Forsaking the esoteric jargon of his profession, Watson called the critics "kooks, shits and incompetents," thus raising the level of discourse to heights not often attained by ordinary mortals.

Eventually, Dean Henry Rosovsky, head of the faculty of arts and sciences, announced that university review committees had approved going ahead with the research and that the Harvard Corporation had authorized funds for construction of the special laboratory. Nevertheless, he sought to allay the fears of those who insisted that it was unwise and unsafe to tamper with nature, saying: "Both committees—and this is the heart of the matter— agree that there are potential hazards, that safe plans are not the same thing as safe execution, and we will not be acting responsibly unless unusual discipline is insisted upon. Consequently, unless the duly constituted committees and safety officers are entirely satisfied, permission to use the facility will not be granted. I say this with the knowledge that our safety record has not always been perfect. We hope to use this opportunity to raise standards of enforcement throughtout the entire science area."

Thus, in spite of continuing opposition from Wald and other scientists, the experiments were launched with a $500,000 grant from the National Institutes of Health, contingent upon the construction of a "special safety laboratory," designated as "P-3," which is only slightly less secure than what the U.S. Army used for its chemical-biological warfare experiments. Some officials at NIH would have recommended ultrasecure laboratories ("P-4") for work with animal tumor viruses or primate cells. One of the two existing P-4 facilities is a white trailer parked inside a barbed-wire corral on the grounds of the National Institutes of Health in Bethesda, Md. It has a "totally sealed environment," with airlocks, decontamination systems, showers for technicians after experiments, and sealed cabinets accessible only through attached gloves. The guidelines in such labs also require the use of "self-destructing, escape-proof microbes" for experiments involving extremely high risks.

But even the most sophisticated safety measures would not pacify the opposition, whose concern has been characterized as "partly philosophical" or even mystical. Sinsheimer, for example, worries about the violation of "nature's evolutionary barrier," which prevents a crossbreeding of different species because of genetic incompatibility. Supporting that view, a Columbia University biochemist, Erwin Chargaff, challengingly asked the proponents of DNA research: "Have we the right to counteract, irreversibly, the evolutionary wisdom of millions of years in order to satisfy the ambition and the curiosity of a few scientists?"

When informed of that query, molecular biologist Stanley Cohen sneeringly commented, "It was Chargaff's evolutionary wisdom that gave us the gene combinations for bubonic plague, smallpox, yellow fever, typhoid, polio and cancer." He further pointed out that man has been tinkering with nature for several centuries, cultivating hybrid plants, crossbreeding animals and creating a host of vaccines and antibiotics. As for the much publicized potential hazards, Bernard Davis, a Harvard Medical School microbiologist, was so confident that the new research would be "perfectly safe" that he publicly offered to drink a tube of recombinant DNA. Declaring that people who predicted monstrous infections were ignoring a long history of safe handling of highly contagious bacteria, Davis emphasized that "those who claim we are letting loose an Andromeda strain are either hysterics or are trying to wreck a whole new field of research."

Whatever the merits of the controversy, it should be noted that Harvard was the focus of much of the media coverage, even though other universities had prior and perhaps more significant DNA research. For example, Herbert Boyer and his colleagues at the University of California (San Francisco) had discovered an extraordinary "cutting enzyme." Unlike the restriction enzymes previously used, this new enzyme did not split apart the twin-stranded DNA with a simple slice. Instead, it created an overlapping, mortise-type fissure that automatically left a single strand of "sticky" DNA at each end, to which new enzymes could be readily attached. Until Boyer's breakthrough discovery, other scientists had to produce these "sticky tails" synthetically.

An equally valuable discovery was made by Professor Stanley Cohen, whose team at Stanford University found a plasmid that had the "uncanny ability to absorb a new gene and thereafter slip into *E. coli.*" When informed of this miraculous "gene conveyer," experimenters throughout the world immediately requested samples for further studies. But because his plasmid (p SC101), when combined with Boyer's enzyme scalpel, so easily facilitated novel gene combinations with possibly dangerous consequences, Dr. Cohen was reluctant to distribute his material. Indeed, this particular situation led to a very private meeting of 104 leading molecular biologists in New Hampshire during the summer of 1973, at which time the assembled scientists voted to ask the National Academy of Scientists to examine the new research techniques for possible risks. They further agreed to express their concern in a public letter that later appeared in *Science*, the nation's most prestigious scientific journal.

Yet, in spite of these earlier developments, which were virtually unknown to anyone outside the closed circle of specialists, DNA research was not a public issue until it suddenly became headline news because of the Harvard–MIT controversy. "When Harvard moved into the picture, it became a hot item," grumbled a resentful California scientist. "The TV networks, the national magazines and big daily newspapers were suddenly fascinated by this tiny *E. coli* bacteria. You would think that Harvard had invented it—that no other university had been involved. But that's not too surprising when you consider how much this country is infected with Harvarditis."

There is, of course, a considerable measure of truth in that accusation, for as I have pointed out elsewhere, the news media have been chronically susceptible to the university's mystique. Whenever there is some novel scientific development elsewhere in the country, news reporters almost automatically "check with Harvard" for confirmation or opposition, as if it were the ultimate authority or academic vatican. When Dr. Linus Pauling and other biochemists began experimenting with megavitamin therapy for schizophrenia (also called orthomolecular psychiatry), reporters consulted with Dr. Seymour Kety, professor of psychiatry at Harvard Medical School. Regarded by younger colleagues as the spiritual father of modern biological psychiatry, Kety expressed skepticism about the new technique, saying that it was a "premature application of inadequate knowledge." He also recalled his first test for a physical cause for schizophrenia in 1948, when he measured the oxygen flow and energy metabolism in the brain and found no differences between the sane and the sick.

"We concluded," he said, "that it takes just as much oxygen to think an irrational thought as to think a rational one. We also concluded that if there was a biochemical disturbance in schizophrenia it probably lay in much more subtle and complex processes."

Pursuing a different approach, Kety and his associates have been trying to determine whether schizophrenia "runs in families" because of genetic inheritance or whether disordered families propel some of the children into similar behavior. Tracing the mental-health histories of children of schizophrenics adopted into normal families and also identical twins separated and raised apart, they have found clear patterns of inheritance of a vulnerability to the disease.

Orthomolecular psychiatrists would probably welcome that premise—but, unlike Kety, they would prescribe heavy doses of certain vitamins and minerals to compensate for "inborn oddities in the metabolism of the brain." They would also predict that, as *The New York Times* reported, "some day soon the Harvard crowd will adopt our theories, and the general public will get the impression that they *invented* vitamin therapy for schizophrenia; they can't lose."

But aside from its primary or secondary (real or imagined) contributions to basic scientific research, the Harvard Medical School has had a significant impact on the teaching and practice of medicine throughout the United States and several foreign countries, as well. It has been estimated that more than 20% of this nation's medical professors received their own professional training at Harvard, many of them serving as deans or department chairmen. They have also distinguished themselves in other fields. Dr. Morris Chafetz, a former professor at HMS, was the first director of the National Institute on Alcohol Abuse and Alcoholism.

Dr. Harry L. Kozol, a 1934 graduate, was the chief psychiatric witness for the prosecution in the trial of Patricia Hearst, in which the district attorney heavily emphasized Kozol's Harvard credentials. He is also the father of Jonathan Kozol, another graduate of Harvard, who won the National Book Award for his best-selling critique of public schools, *Death at an Early Age*.

Of the three doctors appointed by Judge John J. Sirica to examine President Nixon to determine whether he was physically fit to testify in the Watergate trial, two were graduates of the Harvard Medical School: Dr. Charles A. Hufnagel, chairman of the three-man panel, and Dr. Richard Starr Ross. A pioneer in heart surgery and the replacement of diseased heart valves with plastic substitutes, Hufnagel had received the American Heart Association's Distinguished Service Award in 1969.

On a less elevated plane, one should also note the case of Dr. Joseph Beasley, a former professor of population control and family planning at the Harvard School of Public Health, who was convicted in 1975 of conspiring to defraud the federal government of $778,000 in the operation of the Family Health Foundation, a private nonprofit agency that provided birth-control services for poor women in Louisiana. In sentencing the defendant to two years in prison, Judge Alvin Rubin said, "While you portray yourself as a dedicated person whose only interest was in serving the poor, in two and a half years you drew in salary and expenses from Tulane University and the Foundation over $424,000, exclusive of over $50,000 in travel expenses."

One would imagine that a loyal HMS graduate would quickly point out that Dr. Beasley was from the school of public health, which is only an "affiliate" of the more prestigious medical school.

WASHINGTON—Theodore H. White is known to a generation of political reporters as the Boy Scout among the boys on the bus in national campaigns. A famous war and foreign correspondent, best-selling author, he nonetheless wore his eagerness like a press badge. "You'd think," remarked a colleague, "that he was a cub reporter for the Harvard Crimson."
Scrambling came naturally to Teddy White. He grew up Jewish in Boston during the Depression. At an early age, under the eyes of hostile Irish motormen, he was leaping on and off streetcars, selling papers. His family had nothing but a reverence for learning, so Teddy was packed off to Hebrew School, Boston Latin and finally, on a newsboy's scholarship, to Harvard. He was "a meatball"—a day student who brought his own lunch, but was also a scholar, graduating summa cum laude in Chinese history and language.

—Mary McGrory,
*Washington Star* syndicated

## CHAPTER VI

**The Economic Superstars**

## Wide Marijuana and Cocaine Use Reported Among Professionals

### By ROBERT REINHOLD

Special to The New York Times

WASHINGTON, July 21— The use of marijuana and other illicit substances, particularly cocaine, is so widespread among well-educated young professional people with high-pressure jobs that it is increasingly difficult to find any who have not at least tried them.

Dr. Peter G. Bourne, who resigned yesterday as President Carter's adviser on drug abuse after acknowledging that he had written a false drug prescription, said in an interview that he and other members of the White House staff had smoked marijuana and that he was aware of the use of cocaine by some of the President's aides.

"If there were no use of marijuana and cocaine in a group of young people with the kind of educational and social background White House people have, that would characterize them as rather unusual in the United States today," Dr. Lester Grinspoon, a psychiatrist at the Harvard Medical School, said. He is coauthor, with James B. Bakalar, of "Cocaine: A Drug and Its Social Evolution."

"Well, there it is again," said a New York professor when he read the foregoing article. "Whenever something controversial

[103]

pops up, *The New York Times* always contacts some Harvard professor for the most authoritative view of the matter—as if they're the only goddamned authorities in the country!"

"At least it's not John Kenneth Galbraith this time," said another professor. "He's the guy who's usually contacted by reporters when they want an authorative judgment, whether it's on the economic aspects of abortion or a better recipe for Hollandaise sauce. Whatever the hell it is, Big John can always give them an expert opinion on it."

Hoping to get a quantitative measurement of the John Kenneth Galbraith syndrome, in the spring of 1977 we phoned fifty well-known and presumably well-informed Washingtonians (news correspondents, congressmen and top-level government officials) and asked them to name the person whom they considered "the most influential economist" in the country. No less than 68% named Galbraith, the peripatetic scholar-diplomat-author, whose numerous books—including *The Affluent Society* in 1958, *The New Industrial State* in 1967, and *Public Purpose* in 1973—have received much critical attention and best-seller status. Indeed, about 10% of those who named Galbraith were unable to name any other economist, some of them requesting (with no little embarrassment) that we call back so that they might meanwhile dredge up the names of one or two other economists.

But among his colleagues in Harvard's prestigious economics department, which has recently produced four Nobel Prize winners in four successive years, Galbraith is regarded with less esteem. Some call him a popularizer, a facile writer with no great depth, a celebrity rather than a true scholar, while others simply shrug their shoulders or smile enigmatically when asked about Galbraith's reputation beyond the immediate environs of Cambridge. Few, if any, would rank him among the ten or fifteen most distinguished economists, and most certainly would not place him on par with Wassily Leontief, Paul Samuelson, Kenneth Arrow or Simon Smith Kuznets, Harvard's most recent Nobel laureates in economics.

As one might expect, there is a certain ill-disguised envy in some of their appraisals. Seldom able to free themselves of erudite jargon, much of which often seems needlessly involuted and deliberately obscure, academicians have traditionally scoffed at colleagues who can write lucid prose, particularly when it's graced with a shade of humor. So that Galbraith's writing (or most of it) must seem especially offensive to fellow professors whose sober theorizing is confined to the limited readership of the university press or remains in manuscript form, with a few Xeroxed copies for persons within their own small coterie of extremely specialized scholars. Such specialists must inevitably envy Galbraith's ability to translate abstruse theorems into readable language quite often spiced with ironic interpretations, and they are apt to accuse him of simplifying that which cannot be simplified without distortion; but their accusations are generally restrained, soft-voiced, gently ironic, as one would expect from a community that prides itself on the subtlety of its internecine warfare. (As one Harvard professor recently observed, "Our internal struggles are so brutal and nasty because the stakes are so small." To which another professor added, "And because they're the only stakes there are.")

Immersed in extracurricular activities, Galbraith had little time for scholarly research and classroom instruction, all of which was pointedly noted in the student's confidential guide in 1968: "The long ambassador, as he was known affectionately in India, has failed in all of his past courses to demonstrate either economic rigor or an interest in undergraduates." But a year later, the guide was more charitable in its appraisal: "People accustomed to the usual outline form lecture say they find him hard to listen to. But they should get their minds together again; Galbraith is brilliant." That same year, 1969, he gained the esteem of most of the student body when he spearheaded the liberal wing of the faculty in its denunciation of the university administration for calling on local police to break a student strike. Notwithstanding his spirited defense of their right to protest, Galbraith has said that student efforts at educational reform usually lead to a lowering of academic standards, although he believes that the present generation of students is perhaps superior to previous generations. "The most significant change at Harvard," he recently observed, "has been the conversion of its undergraduates from a slightly ludicrous aristocracy to a somewhat serious meritocracy."

In their ambivalent evaluation of his intellectual achievement, Galbraith's students seem to echo a corresponding ambivalence among his fellow faculty, but some of his colleagues have found considerable merit in his scholarly endeavors. Leontief, for example, recently remarked that "as economic theory has gotten narrower, Galbraith has provided a bridge to the real world."

Nevertheless, neither Leontief nor any other serious student of economics would be apt to say that Galbraith has produced original and seminal work, the kind of research that might affect the fundamental structure of an economic system and perhaps earn the much-coveted Nobel Prize. In that respect he has been overshadowed by at least four Harvard economists who, though much less celebrated, have engaged in basic research and experimentation that may indeed alter economic functions within this country and/or between nations elsewhere. Citing their specific contributions to the field of economics, the Nobel selection committee made the following comments:

1970

Paul A. Samuelson

> pour les travaux par lesquels il a développé la théorie économique statique et dynamique et a activement contribué à faire monter le niveau d'analyse dans la science économique.

1971

Simon Kuznets

> pour son interprétation de la croissance économique, interprétation fondée empiriquement, qui a ouvert la voie à une pénétration nouvelle et plus profonde de la structure économique et sociale et des processus de développement.

1972

Kenneth J. Arrow (and John R. Hicks of England)

> de l'Université Harvard, Cambridge, Mass., Etats-Unis, pour leurs contributions fondamentales à la théorie générale d'équilibre économique et à la théorie du mieux-être.

1973

Wassily Leontief

> de l'Université de Harvard, Cambridge, Mass., Etats-Unis, pour le développement de la methode de l'input-output et son application à des problèmes économiques importants.

It would be difficult, indeed impossible, adequately to appraise the combined and cumulative contribution of these four men to government policies and commercial-industrial decisions in this country and throughout the world during and after their association with Harvard. They have also profoundly influenced hundreds of graduate students who have subsequently served in government agencies, private enterprise or university faculties in the United States and abroad (for Harvard has always attracted an international student body), thus influencing thousands of future government administrators, congressmen, state legislators, private businessmen and even more professors of economics—a geometric progression of men and women who occupy positions that directly or indirectly affect the economic lives of all of us. But in order to get at least a minimal notion of the far-ranging influence of each of these Nobel laureates, we might briefly review their respective fields of expertise:

Paul Samuelson's work in economic theory has been in modern welfare economics, linear programming, Keynesian economics, economic dynamics, international trade theory, logic choice and maximization. "In this age of specialization, I sometimes think of myself as the 'last generalist' in economics," he once wrote.

His *Economics: An Introductory Analysis,* first published in 1948, has become the best-selling economics textbook of all time. The textbook has sold more than a million copies and has been translated into French, German, Italian, Hungarian, Polish, Korean, Portuguese, Spanish and Arabic. It is now in its fifth edition. "The book's emphasis on different themes has changed with the changing of the nation's economic problems," wrote *Business Week* in 1959. "The first edition was dominated by the end-of-the-war worry that widespread unemployment would return....later editions put growing stress on fiscal and monetary controls over inflation. In the later editions Samuelson has worked toward what he calls a 'neoclassical synthesis' of ancient and modern economic findings. Briefly, his synthesis is that nations today can successfully control either depression or inflation by fiscal and monetary policies....Some economists feel that Samuelson's book...is really his greatest contribution. It has gone a long way toward giving the world a common economic language."

Simon Kuznets has devoted most of his scholarly efforts to achieving a quantitative precision of economic data which seem relevant to an understanding of the processes of social change. Having collected an extraordinarily large body of statistical material which he has analyzed with a shrewd and penetrating intelligence, he has shed new light on economic growth. Thus, among other things, he has developed methods for calculating the size of the changes in national income, attaining numerical projections whenever possible and also elucidating "the margin of uncertainty" and the indeterminateness which arises from changes in consumption and production. In so doing, Kuznets has made use of models which demonstrate the interrelation of strategic elements in an economic system, but he has consistently avoided abstract and generalizing models which provide only limited opportunities for empirical testing.

Wassily Leontief's most notable contribution is his so-called "input-output method," which is a mathematically and statistically formulated model designed to capture in empirical analysis the complicated interdependence within the production process.

Since a modern economy produces thousands (even millions) of different commodities and services, most of which are used directly or indirectly as inputs in the production of other commodities and services, it is obviously difficult to calculate how large a production of various commodities is necessary for any desired quantity of specific goods or services, or to calculate the effect of such production on all other elements of the economy. In order to analyze these complicated, mutual interdependences within a production system, Leontief devised a method that is now used for economic forecasting and planning by various national governments and by industrial conglomerates as well.

For example, in connection with the disarmament in the United States after the Second World War and with the rearmament for the Korean War, his input-output method was used to determine how such disarmament and rearmament would influence the production volume and employment level in various sectors of the American economy, taking into account also the various indirect effects on demand for inputs within the defense industry and in other enterprises directly or indirectly delivering commodities and services to the defense industry. (It should also be mentioned that Leontief's system was used by the U.S. Air Force in World War II to determine which industrial targets in Germany would yield "the biggest bang for the buck.")

Unfortunately, Leontief's forty-four-year tenure at Harvard came to a bitter end in 1975 when he resigned a year ahead of schedule for reasons that still remain unclear. For several years he had called for the "disenfranchisement" of tenured professors who had failed to give adequate attention to students and also strongly proposed the appointment of certain young instructors with a Marxist orientation so as to broaden the scope of instruction in the economics department. And he was particularly displeased when the university failed to give a tenured appointment to one of his assistants. Though acknowledging

Leontief's "stated reasons" for his much-publicized resignation (*The New York Times* reported it on the front page), some of his colleagues quietly voice the suspicion that "he deeply resented not having been appointed University Professor," a position held by only five professors at any given time.

Shortly before Leontief's resignation, a special Visiting Committee (composed of leading economists not presently affiliated with Harvard) had issued a report criticizing the department of economics for "the narrowness of its approach" and for "the deterioration in attitudes and relationships within the department." Both the report and Leontief's parting criticism were applauded by many of the graduate economics students, generally regarded as among the world's most promising scholars. Although undergraduates had complained now and then about the quality of their instruction, some graduate students had bitterly complained about faculty absenteeism, poor teaching by senior professors and the dismissal of four radical instructors who *were* good teachers.

Student dissension had become so acute that in the fall of 1974 the Graduate Economics Club felt compelled to write a warning letter to the entering class of doctoral-degree candidates. "In general," said the letter, "most of us have found that the first year at Harvard was the worst year of our lives. The teaching is terrible, the professors distant and uninterested in new students."

A similar view was expressed in a comment attached to the report of the Visiting Committee. "As things stand," said one member, "I would not advise a bright senior to go to Harvard for graduate study in economics unless he was of such specialized interest and talent that he clearly could become a student protégé of one of the giants of the economics department."

But, as anyone who has done graduate work at Harvard will attest, this is not a new or novel condition. The graduate school faculties have always catered to the specially gifted students. And like all other branches of the university, the economics department has for years tried to attract the best economists in the world for its tenured faculty, thus acquiring a collection of independent superstars, in the words of the Visiting Committee member, "intent on their research, their consulting jobs with government or business—and, lastly, on their teaching."

Unfortunately, according to Henry Rosovsky, dean of the faculty of arts and sciences and also professor of economics, the university can do very little to reshuffle the priorities of its superstars. "You just don't call in a Harvard professor and say why don't you teach better," said the dean to a visiting reporter.

But in the wake of Leontief's angry resignation, the department revised parts of the graduate curriculum and put new emphasis on classroom performance. The faculty also formally voted to make teaching ability a major criterion for future appointments, along with such criteria as research and publication in learned journals.

"If only we could get another Schumpeter," said one faculty member with a wistful sigh, "an intellectual giant *who could also teach*. With this new cloning process, we could multiply him by ten every generation, so all the rest of us could sit on our ass and let the Schumpies do all the teaching."

He was referring, of course, to Joseph Schumpeter, whose classroom lectures in the '30s and '40s continuously captivated thousands of students with generous portions of urbane wit and penetrating analysis. Within their first few days in Cambridge, graduate students were sure to hear the familiar tale that at the age of eighteen Schumpeter had decided to become the world's greatest economist, the world's greatest lover and the world's greatest horseman—but that he had somehow failed to accomplish his third goal.

Upon his death in 1950, several of his colleagues contributed to a memorial collection of essays on Schumpeter's contributions to the social sciences. Among them was Paul A. Samuelson, who wrote the following:

There were many Schumpeters: the brilliant *enfant terrible* of the Austrian School who before the age of thirty had written two great books; the young Cairo lawyer with a stable of horses; the Austrian Finance Minister; the social philosopher and prophet of capitalist development; the historian of economic doctrine; the economic theorist espousing use of more exact methods and tools of reasoning; the teacher of economics. . . . You might say of Schumpeter that, although he had an absolute advantage both as a scholar and a personality, his comparative advantage was if anything almost greater as a personality. His books speak for themselves, but only his pupils can recapture the impact of his colorful personality. . . .

There was in him a consciousness of great powers, and this served as an irritant urging him toward creative activity. . . . this feeling of great personal powers was of course of tremendous importance in connection with his professional work. It also showed itself in every aspect of his life: he was quite prepared to talk expertly on anything from Etruscan Art to medieval law; to read, or feel that he could read, Italian, Dutch, and Scandinavian; to outline a theory of metaphysics. This lack of inhibition was extremely important in giving him the freedom to make daring and interesting sociological hypotheses concerning phenomena on the fringes of politics and economics.

The one field in which he did show real humility was in connection with mathematics—a statement that may be surprising to some. It is true that he never tired of pointing out to the non-mathematical the virtues for economics of mathematics. It is also true that he would often refer with a wave of his hand to quite difficult problems as if they were elementary and easy. But nonetheless he was quite aware of his own lack of facility with mathematics and cheerfully admitted the difficulties he had in mastering and retaining mathematical techniques.

I think to the end he regarded it as a slightly mystical fact that a mixed-difference-differential equation of the Frisch-Tinbergen type involves complex exponentials which in a miraculous manner give rise to sinusoidal periodicities. . . ."

Professor Samuelson's encomium has been quoted at some length for two reasons: first of all, because it expresses a genuine appreciation of Schumpeter's genius as a teacher; second, because it's a prime example of the fiendishly erudite put-downs one is apt to encounter in the higher echelons of the Harvard community, where praise is seldom complete or unmixed—and is often a handy vehicle for a circuitous demonstration of the praiser's own superiority.

Whatever his shortcomings, Schumpeter was a giant among giants in a department that enjoyed a worldwide reputation for all-round excellence—a reputation that developed into a mystique when its faculty and graduates began to permeate the New Deal administration of Franklin D. Roosevelt, who readily accepted their espousal of the "deficit spending" theories of John Meynard Keynes. There were so many Harvard economists commuting from Cambridge to Washington that some critics (particularly news columnists like Westbrook Pegler) expressed dark suspicions about a secret tunnel between the White House and the Yard. Perhaps the most celebrated commuter was Professor Alvin Hansen, whose devotion to Keynesian principles was a bit too zealous for some of his less reverent colleagues.

"I can't worship Alvin's god," said a young instructor. "I have my own god—and his name is Schumpeter on Mondays and Leontief on Wednesdays."

Interestingly enough, while most of their fellow professors became full-salaried absentees with generous consulting fees from government agencies and private industries, Schumpeter and Leontief usually showed up for their classes and earned high praise for their brilliant teaching from grateful students, many of whom seldom saw any other professors.

For those who remember the scarcity of good teachers in that fabled "golden era," the complaints of modern-day graduate students are mere redescriptions of a situation that probably has always existed in a department forever proud of its superscholars, each one of them secure in his lifetime tenure and fully confident that no department chairman or dean would dare to suggest that he improve his teaching or get out. Indeed, some of these innately shy, distracted, incorrigibly introverted scholars could never have been good teachers. (How well I remember a course with Sumner Schlicter, an absolutely brilliant scholar and writer, whose twice-a-week lectures were a series of half-finished sentences...long, suspenseful pauses...vague elliptical allusions to Weber's vector analysis or Modigliani's "envelope curve"... sudden lapses into deep silence...then mumbled phrases and half-whispers spoken only to someone inside himself as he stared out the window at an invisible audience perched on the elm tree next to Emerson Hall. My notes for his course on collective bargaining were as puzzling as excerpts from *Finnegan's Wake*.)

Leontief, by contrast, was so gently provocative and stimulating in his lectures that his students would frequently applaud as he left the room, an accolade generally reserved for a professor's last lecture of the course.

But Leontief is gone, and so are Simon Kuznets, his fellow Nobel Prize winner; Alexander Gerschenkron, economics historian; Edward S. Mason, the development expert; and John Kenneth Galbraith. But they have been replaced over the past few years by Kenneth J. Arrow (another Nobel Prize winner), Dale W. Jorgenson, Harvey Liebenstein, Zvi Griliches and three well-known former members of the Council of Economic Advisers in Washington—Otto Eckstein, James S. Dusenberry and Hendrik S. Houthakker.

As previously stated, some of the current superstars are considered unsatisfactory performers in the classroom. One exception is Leibenstein, the population expert, whose wry humor is a relaxing counterpoint to the penetrating questions that often jolt his students into a nervous awareness. As one of them recently observed, "You can't always tell whether he's joking or jabbing—or both."

Another notable exception to the poor-teacher syndrome is Professor Eckstein, whose course in freshman economics usually attracts more than 800 students. But Eckstein is exceptional in an even more dramatic way: he is also a fantastically successful businessman, who had made himself a multimillionaire in scarcely eight years. He is the cofounder, president and largest shareholder of Data Resources, Inc., which has served more than 550 clients—including two-thirds of the nation's largest manufacturers, most of the big banks, scores of brokerage firms, utilities companies, state agencies, foreign governments and corporations, the U.S. Departments of State, Treasury, Commerce and Justice and at least two dozen other federal agencies. At any time of day or night, there are constant dialogues between DRI and 80 to 125 of its clients (by way of long-distance phone lines), with Eckstein's giant Burroughs 7700 computer whirring out answers to questions that range from "What is the price of avocados in Alaska?" to the probable effects of broad economic trends on specific products. Answers to these and thousands of other questions are provided instantly by DRI, which has accumulated by far the world's largest bank of economic statistics—more than 3.6 million series of figures about the United States and 127 other countries. Eckstein's staff of 250 economists and analysts constantly update these data from huge masses of statistics provided free by governments, associations and corporations, all of which are fed into the most capacious computer ever built by Burroughs. Based on thousands of mathematical equations derived from such data, Eckstein's econometric models produce overall forecasts of growth, inflation, interest rates and the like. They also produce thousands of "micro forecasts" for specific industries and products, with predictions changing as new indicators spew from the computer or when major political events occur. Thus, within seventy-two hours after the Arab oil embargo was imposed, DRI was able to forecast how much insurance companies' profits would increase due to a projected decline in driving and auto accidents.

Fees for such prophecies—augmented by retainers for personal consultations and other services—have produced steadily increasing revenues for Data Resources, Inc. With a gross income of $17 million in 1977 (a 35% rise over the previous year), its profits climbed 70% to $1,502,000. Since DRI went public in 1976, its shares have risen from $11.50 to $18, thus bucking the bear market and giving Eckstein a stake in excess of $4 million—which, as *Time* magazine commented, "is not bad for a college professor who didn't go into business until he was past the age of forty."

Wistfully alluding to Eckstein's enormous financial success, a much poorer fellow professor said, "I'd like to ask Otto for a job, but I'm afraid he knows that I get awful nervous around those damned computers, especially when they're processing *real* data from the *real* business world. I'm much more comfortable with all that make-believe data we get from the government—the kind of stuff you can feed a computer like cotton candy."

Aside from the incalculable impact on governmental policies and business practices by members of the economics faculty (Eckstein, Dusenberry, Jorgenson, Houthakker, *et al.*), hundreds of Harvard graduates and former professors have profoundly influenced the economic life of this country and numerous foreign countries.

Among the more eminent Harvard-trained economists is Alice Rivlin, director of the Congressional Budget Office, which she has headed since it was first formed in 1975. Possessed of a keen analytical mind that functions with computer precision, Ms. Rivlin has often antagonized critics with her cool, occasionally defiant independence. Her CBO staff of 208 economists and other specialists was organized to analyze tax and spending options for all federal agencies—from welfare to defense—and to assess the probable costs of each proposed program, as well as its probably impact on the rest of the economy. Where the Congress had previously groped blindly in passing hundreds of appropriation bills with no real estimate of their cost, it can now set spending ceilings and sometimes cut budgets to stay under them. But on certain occasions, Ms. Rivlin has ruffled the feathers of the Democratic leaders who hired her.

For example, when her CBO staff estimated that savings on oil imports would be closer to 3.5 million barrels daily by 1985 rather than the 4.5 million projected by the president, Ms. Rivlin told reporters, "There's been a lot of talk about sacrifice, but one doesn't see it here."

Incensed by her remark, House Speaker Tip O'Neill and representative Robert Giaimo, chairman of the House Budget Committee, angrily confronted Rivlin and warned her to shut up in public. "Who do you think you're working for anyway?" asked Giaimo. "Congress or the general public?"

"Both," said Rivlin, her dark eyes blazing.

Later, in an off-the-record remark to a reporter, a congressional aide described her as "stubborn and arrogant," then smilingly added, "but Harvard people are all that way—and worse when they're female."

That all-inclusive condemnation, so often repeated that it has become a cliche, would hardly apply to Barry B. Bosworth, a former Harvard professor, who was appointed by President Carter as chief of the Council on Wage and Price Stability. Quietly confident but in no sense arrogant, Bosworth initially supported the administration's cautious approach to inflation, but soon thereafter urged that the council play a more aggressive role in the campaign against spiraling costs of living. To provide the White House with a graphic picture of inflation, Bosworth and his staff began keeping an "early warning index," a day-to-day chart of price and cost developments in a few bellwether industries such as construction, auto manufacturing and steel production.

"In the past," said Bosworth, "the council churned out studies and recommendations that may have been good but went nowhere. My job is to see that our work gets transmitted more effectively."

Although Bosworth earned his Ph.D. in economics at the University of Michigan, his Cambridge connection is more apt to be mentioned by television and newspaper reporters. And some of the people around the White House offhandedly refer to him as "one of our Harvard brains."

WASHINGTON—Samuel P. Huntington, scholar, militarist and thorn in the side of world communism, returned to Harvard this month. Behind him in the world of Washington policymaking he left a carefully primed bear trap that could snap shut on Soviet-American trade if the Russians continue to push Jimmy Carter.

The bear trap lies buried in new regulations that bring the National Security Council into the review of export licenses for American technology being sold to the Soviet Union and other communist countries.

The new review procedures, in turn, grow out of a secret study memorandum that Huntington and other National Security Council staffers have been working on for months and which helped structure President Carter's decision last month to use trade restrictions to demonstrate his displeasure with Soviet actions.

—Jim Hoagland,
*Washington Post* syndicate

# CHAPTER VII Harvard and the CIA Elite

IN THE SPRING OF 1978 *The New York Times* reported that Derek Bok, the president of Harvard, had asked the Central Intelligence Agency to cease its recruiting of students at the university—either openly or secretly.

Dale Peterson, a spokesman for the CIA, said in response that "basically what you have are two institutions—Harvard and the CIA—with overlapping interests." He said that whatever the intelligence agency was doing at Harvard was "legal" and that he thought the disgreement had reached a point at which "it is up to Congress to arbitrate it."

The conflict was highlighted in a series of letters exchanged by Mr. Bok and Admiral Stansfield Turner, CIA director.

"As it is," Admiral Turner wrote on May 15, "The restraints which we have already imposed on ourselves in this area have on occasion limited the capability of the intelligence community. Any further extension of the restrictions to effectively rule out the two types of activities in question is neither legally required nor is otherwise advisable in light of the potential obstacles which such actions would pose."

Admiral Turner insisted, "We cannot consider this agency bound by any set of procedures in which Harvard singles out the CIA." But Mr. Bok was equally emphatic in saying, "There is a question of whether an agency of Government can take it upon itself to simply disregard, in secret, the rules that a private institution has developed for itself." And in testimony before the Senate Select Committee on Intelligence, he implored Congress to "make it clear that these activities cannot continue and that the internal rules of academic institutions should be respected."

The Harvard president expressed particular concern about the possibility of professors—on behalf of the CIA—recruiting as future spies foreign students who would be asked to work for the agency upon returning to their home countries.

But the CIA spokesman, Mr. Peterson, complained, "The intelligence community is being singled out by Harvard. No such guidelines have been made to cover corporations or other organizations functioning on Harvard's campus. The bulk of our activities at Harvard and elsewhere are open. There are, however, some things done clandestinely, and this is where the problem is. We try to use these activities in as limited a fashion as possible. But they aren't illegal and you can't arbitrarily rule them out.

"Our problem," he added, "is that on campus there is a stigma when anyone deals with the intelligence organizations. But there are people willing to do it, and if everyone who makes contact with us has to report it, our sources will dry up."

Since secret recruiting is by definition secret, there is no way of ascertaining whether the agency has ever acceded to Bok's request. In any event, President Bok would have had no difficulty conveying his sentiments to the CIA, whose deputy director for national intelligence, Robert R. Bowie, is also a Harvard man. Indeed the agency has always been staffed at the upper levels by an Ivy League elite, "by the right people looking out for one another's sons and friends."

Bowie, formerly a professor of government at Harvard, had

been directly and indirectly associated with the intelligence agency since it was initially organized in 1950—at which time William L. Langer, a Harvard professor of history, served as head of the agency's Board of National Estimates. There is no published estimate of the number of Harvard graduates they recruited for "Langley Hall," but it was certainly substantial. And their efforts in this regard were no doubt enhanced by the fact that a fellow alumnus, William Bundy, was deputy director of the CIA.

A long-time protégé of Allen Dulles, the older Bundy brother had a remarkable career in government, but he always seemed to live in the shadow of his younger sibling—this despite the fact that William was an honor graduate of the Harvard Law School, while McGeorge had never attained a graduate degree in any field. But as one critic sized them up: "Bill was not as quick as Mac, and not as open. Mac had competed in the somewhat more open environment of Harvard, where sheer brains counted, whether they were immigrant brains, blue-collar brains or WASP brains; and he had triumphed there, his connections not hurting him a bit. But the process had ventilated him (Mac knew the value of a Kaysen or Wiesner), and he liked brains for brains' sake, whereas Bill had made his way up through the more closed profession of the inner bureaucracy, particularly the CIA, where connections and birthrights were far more important."

Aside from their maternal connections to the supra-Harvard Lowell family, the Bundy brothers had a father who was a graduate of the Harvard Law School and a protégé of Chief Justice Holmes and Harold Stimson; and William was married to the daughter of Dean Acheson. But although he had Harvard in his genes and in his pores, William Bundy somehow failed to get into the inner-inner circles of the Kennedy-Johnson administrations, where his younger brother Mac played a major role. In fact, he was always called "that other Bundy" by Lyndon Johnson, who frequently professed having trouble with people's names when he wanted to put them down. Kissinger, for example, became Schlesinger; and Dick Goodwin became Good*man*.

His puckish name confusion was aimed mostly at Harvard men, which probably reflected Johnson's underlying sense of inferiority with respect to the university. A prime example of this appears in Doris Kearns' *Lyndon Johnson and the American Dream*, which records a conversation between her and LBJ, in which he asks her to help him write his memoirs:

"Of course I will," I said.
There was a long pause and then: "Thanks, thanks a lot. Now you take care of yourself up there at Harvard. Don't let them get at you, for God's sake, don't let their hatred for Lyndon Johnson poison your feelings about me."

Later in the book there is a further comment regarding LBJ's persistent requests that she join him in Texas: "But I was a teacher at Harvard, already a member of that inner group which wrote the books and which, he firmly believed, shaped the final verdict of history."

Sam Houston Johnson, the president's younger brother, has always believed that "Lyndon's fancy-pants Harvard advisers" shaped a disastrous verdict in the Vietnam War—that Lyndon was too much in awe of their "supposed intelligence," and that he should have fired "that whole Harvard gang" when he took office after the Kennedy assassination. Upon the publication of his controversial book *My Brother Lyndon* (written in collaboration with this author), Sam appeared on the David Frost television show and repeated his charge that Lyndon had been overly impressed by the Cambridge contingent. "Hell," said Sam, "he even started talking like them—got himself a Harvard accent, so you couldn't hardly understand him anymore."

Although only a sharp-eared linguist from Texas would be able to detect this subtle change in Lyndon Johnson's speech, there can be no doubt that he was heavily influenced by advisers originally recruited by John Kennedy. The incestuousness of this group is graphically illustrated in the following excerpt from

David Halberstam's *The Best and the Brightest,* in which the movers and shakers are involved in behind-the-scenes maneuvers to get Senate approval of a treaty on nuclear weapons: "... So Mac Bundy's deputy, Carl Kaysen, got together with Abe Chayes, the State Department's legal adviser, and with Mc-Naughton, who was an expert on arms control, and decided that their instincts about being worried were good ones. They went back to McNamara and spelled out their doubts; he listened for a few moments and then said—I agree, you're right and I was wrong; it is more serious, and you're now the committee to oversee the executive branch's argument. McNaughton is the chief, and you're to put together our case, check out who the witnesses are, and balance the record."

*All of the five men mentioned in the above passage were from Harvard—and most of their subordinates were also from Cambridge.*

When I showed this excerpt to a UCLA professor, his reaction was quick and pithy: "That simply proves that Harvard breeds more famous fools, and that they often conspire together to compound their foolishness."

But our policies in Vietnam were not simply mere foolishness—they were tragic blunders of monumental dimensions, blunders conceived and carried out by men whose intellectual capacities were presumably of a high order, whose self-assurance verged on arrogance. Still, there were a few who eventually came to doubt the wisdom of their own sophisticated machinations.

One such person was John McNaughton, once described as "the classic rationalist," who prided himself on always being able to distinguish between illusion and reality. While teaching a course on evidence at the Harvard Law School, he had often used an amusing gambit to show his students the difference between fact and fantasy. He would suddenly draw a water pistol from his briefcase and splash one of the students, then he'd quickly ask several other students to give a detailed account of what had happened, often getting ten or fifteen versions of this fairly simple incident. Later on, in meetings at the Defense Department, he sadly noted that high-ranking generals and bureaucrats were equally unable to see or hear clearly—or that they saw and heard only what they *wanted* to see and hear. And being possessd of prodigious memory and a gift for mimickry, he would sometimes entertain his staff with word-by-word replays of a particular meeting, thereby revealing the prejudices and self-protecting lies of some of the participants. Thus, as one writer remarked, "he was a brilliant bureaucratic gossip." He was also (most of the time) a cool-headed analyst, who could study a problem with complete detachment, almost always submerging his own prejudices in his search for facts and logic.

Though he was McNamara's most respected deputy, McNaughton's brusque, impatient manner occasionally annoyed the Pentagon brass, some of whom sensed a hint of Harvardian disdain in his badgering questions about strategy and costs. Others felt that he was not hawkish enough for the position he held. As a proud-to-be-what-I-am midwesterner, he was not of the eastern elite that embraced a hard line on national security, containment in Europe, the arms race, nuclear deterrence, and the domino theory. "From the moment he entered the Defense Department," says Halberstam, "he had begun to question the widsom of some of America's commitments, what were considered then the realities of foreign policy and are now considered the myths. The young men around him, who were schooled in the language and litany of the Cold War, regarded him with certain misgivings. Wasn't this a kind of Midwestern isolationism showing? Wasn't it too bad that McNaughton hadn't taken the right graduate courses with Kissinger and the others so he would *know* about these things, as they knew."

Nevertheless, he was ambitious enough to accept the establishment "widsom" and soon became one of the most efficient cogs in the Pentagon machine, deftly and tirelessly applying his analytical skills to the multiple demands of the war in Vietnam. He was so totally driven that it caused some concern among his colleagues and friends. One of them was Roger Fisher, a

Harvard Law School classmate, who had once been squeezed into McNaughton's tight schedule for an exceedingly quick lunch between 12:35 and 12:45 on the dot. As they half-swallowed their previously ordered sandwiches, Fisher noted the "killer schedule" on McNaughton's desk calendar and urged him to ease up, to push aside the heaps of paperwork and to sit back and reflect on the ultimate objectives of American policy. (Himself a bit dovish, Fisher also hoped that his old friend would give some thought to how the United States wanted Hanoi to react.) But McNaughton seemed impatient with his visitor's suggestions. "Look at my schedule," he said, as if there were no time for philosophical ruminations. And when Fisher finally took a good second look at the schedule, with its long series of five- and ten-minute tasks and appointments, he saw a blocked-out space of five hours—from 1:15 to 6:15—with a scrawled notation: *"What are we trying to get Hanoi to do?"**

But whatever his doubts about U.S. involvement in Vietnam, McNaughton remained a gung-ho participant in the planning and execution of military strategy, expressing his doubts only to McNamara, who was also increasingly (but secretly) dubious about the administration's policies. Thus, the two top officials in the Defense Department deliberately concealed their doubts from Lyndon Johnson (and the American public) while advising him to pursue and expand a cruel and devastating war that never seemed to end.

Yet painfully aware of possible failure, McNaughton secretly assigned Daniel Ellsberg (also from Harvard) to prepare a White Paper that would rationalize American withdrawal from Vietnam—if everything should begin to collapse. This was in late 1964, when the war hawks were in complete control, and McNaughton fully realized the political risks of even thinking

---

*Fisher, incidentally, was the young lawyer who was red-baited by Senator Joseph McCarthy during the televised McCarthy–Army hearings, a tactic that prompted attorney Joseph Welch to utter his memorable retort to McCarthy: "My God, man, is there no shred of decency in you?"

like a dove. Consequently, he pledged Ellsberg to absolute secrecy, ordering him not to discuss the project with anyone else in their shop, and to type the report himself so that not even a secretary would learn its contents. "You should be clear," he warned Ellsberg, "that you could be signing the death warrant to your career by having anything to do with calculations and decisions like these. A lot of people have been ruined for less."

McNaughton's own continuing ambivalence increased as Ellsberg showed him initial drafts of his report; but, knowing that McNamara did not yet fully share his feelings, McNaughton carefully avoided expressing any doubts about a particular matter unless he had substantial corroboration from an independent source. He was no doubt aware of his boss' negative reaction to Desmond FitzGerald (another Harvard graduate and the number-four man at the CIA), who was assigned to give McNamara weekly briefings on Vietnam. Time and again, the data-obsessed secretary of defense would ask FitzGerald for more and more numbers to support this or that opinion—till finally one afternoon in 1964 FitzGerald bluntly told him that most of the statistics were wrong or meaningless, that the situation "just doesn't smell right, and we're in for a lot rougher time than any of us want to believe." Apparently not wanting to hear anything contrary to his daily bombs-away advice to President Johnson and his White House staff, McNamara curtly ended the discussion and let it be known that he wanted no more briefings from FitzGerald.

Aware of McNamara's unpredictable behavior and not wishing to overburden him with his own ever-increasing doubts, McNaughton began to confide in Michael Forrestal, a most discreet fellow graduate of the Harvard Law School, who was a top adviser at the White House. They had worked together in administering the Marshall Plan under the direction of their former professor, Milton Katz. (Two of their fellow administrators were also Katz protégés, Elliot Richardson and Kingman Brewster.) Comforted by that old-school tie, they would have long soul-searching discussions about their participation in a "wrong war," always meeting in a clandestine manner at some distance from the Pentagon—then they would resume their roles as obedient and ambitious hawks.

Eventually, as history has well recorded, it was Ellsberg who finally came out of the doves' closet and delivered the Pentagon Papers to *The New York Times* and other newspapers, thus revealing the secrets that McNaughton had once warned him not to tell anyone. Shocked and angry, administration officials unsuccessfully tried to muzzle the press, while opponents of the war immediately proclaimed Ellsberg a new national hero. He was especially appreciated in Cambridge, where students and professors alike had long resented the disproportionately large numbers of prominent prowar government officials from Harvard. In a pardonable mixture of metaphors, a young sophomore proudly announced that "a Harvard dove has shot down the fucking Harvard hawks."

But the hawks mentioned in the Pentagon Papers were the old ones from the Kennedy-Johnson administrations, and Richard Nixon had already drafted his own hawk from the very same aviary, Professor Henry Kissinger.

Most knowledgeable observers know that the university has been deply involved in the foreign affairs of this country for many years, directly and indirectly—but some may not realize the degree to which that involvement has been institutionalized. Perhaps a brief review of the histories and activities of a few in-house organizations will provide a clearer picture of Harvard's considerable influence in "the world out there,"

## The Center for International Affairs

The university's much-publicized Center for International Affairs was established in 1957, during McGeorge Bundy's regime as dean of the college, but the principal initiative for the center came from Robert R. Bowie, who was then serving as assistant secretary of state under John Foster Dulles. Indeed, as a former professor at Harvard, Bowie happily agreed to return to Cambridge as the center's first director.

Among those who helped him organize and finance his brainchild were such old friends as Bundy; Dean Rusk, then director of the Rockefeller Foundation and later president of Cornell University; Don Price, a Ford Foundation official who was later dean of the Kennedy School of Government; Henry Kissinger and Thomas Schelling, both professors in the department of government; and Professor Raymond Vernon of the law school.

Although this brain trust was subsequently regarded by the press as a unique group put together at the request of John F. Kennedy, it had been functioning for at least three years before his election to the presidency. With ample funding from private foundations, the center provided a congenial ambiance for academic researchers and governmental officials with an identity of purpose in international affairs. The scope of their interests and potential influence can be readily discerned in a letter to Dean Ford from Benjamin Brown (dated January 3, 1967) regarding one of several projects funded by the Foundation in subsequent years:

> The Cambridge group that I told you about on the telephone have decided to try to organize over the next three years a series of bilateral U.S.-Japanese meetings on international security and related matters of common concern to the two countries. The meetings would renew and enlarge the contacts made by the Americans who went to Japan under Harvard/Carnegie Endowment auspices last April.
>
> We think that intellectual contacts with the Japanese on security matters are of special importance in the present period.... The "quietism" that marked the Japanese mood in the fifteen or so years after the war seems to have passed....With a growing confidence and sense of their potentialities many Japanese are beginning to think about augmenting their influence in Asian and Pacific affairs....
>
> Our group includes at present Ed Reischauer, John Lindbeck and

Dwight Perkins of the East Asian Center at Harvard; Ed Gullion and Marshall Shulman of the Fletcher School; Paul Doty, Chairman of the American Academy Committee which has been conducting the arms control talks with the Soviets, Europeans and Indians; and Tom Schelling, Henry Kissinger, Abe Halperin and myself of the Center for International Affairs.

The three-year budget which is enclosed comes to $150,000. We hope that the Ford Foundation will contribute $100,000 toward this, and we will try to pick up the balance from the Johnson Foundation at Racine, Wisconsin....

We have informally discussed the project with officers of the State Department and ACDA, who agree as to its importance. There is every indication that ACDA would be prepared to make a substantial contribution to the budget but for reasons which you will understand we are of the opinion that private financing would be preferable....

The Harvard Center for International Affairs has been frequently confused with the Center for International Studies at MIT, perhaps because the latter institute is really a joint enterprise of both schools. Indeed, according to a confidential memorandum, "much of the initiative for the establishment of the Center came from members of the Harvard faculty. It has been conceived of from the beginning, in all substantive respects, as a cooperative venture serving the interests of the entire Cambridge community."

But as one scans the list of people on the Center's advisory boards, one gets the distinct impression that the interests served may have exceeded those of the Cambridge community:

*Advisory Board*
Paul Buck, Harvard University
Edward S. Mason, Harvard University
Julius A. Stratton, MIT
John E. Burchard, MIT
Henry M. Wriston, Brown University
*Advisory Board on Soviet Bloc Studies*
Charles Bohlen, U.S. Department of State

Allen Dulles, CIA
Philip E. Mosely, Columbia University
Leslie G. Stevens, vice Admiral, U.S. Navy, retired

The center had its origins in a number of attempts to mobilize the intellectual and academic resources of the Cambridge community with respect to certain issues posed by the cold war. These organizational efforts were prompted and/or encouraged by Washington officials previously associated with Harvard and MIT, who were particularly interested in devising techniques for penetrating the Iron Curtain with ideas from the noncommunist world. There were, however, certain skeptics who detected more devious motives, and some of their skepticism was expressed in an editorial published in the *Crimson,* the Harvard student newspaper: "We are not even dealing with the question whether a university can justifiably devote some of its resources to advising the government; we are dealing with institutions that provide academic cover for completely prostituted scholarship, a scholarship whose entire purpose is the strengthening of the foreign policies of the U.S."

It was later revealed that the CIA was one of the primary (but secret) sources of funds for the MIT center from its inception in 1951. As one critic commented, "... the CIA has been one of the easier agencies for liberal scholars to work with. Its China specialists, for example, are widely recognized as the brightest researchers in government. Protected by a shield of invisibility, CIA researchers can believe and express the kinds of heresies for which State Department researchers can be fired. Consequently, the CIA has been one of the most innovative of government agencies in paying for dissenting, imaginative research."

## The Development Advisory Service

Economists at Harvard have access to an in-house agency for producing development programs for countries of the Third

World, the Development Advisory Service, established in 1962. Known within the department of economics as DAS, this organization was an outgrowth of advisory work conducted by Professor Edward Mason as early as 1954, when he directed an eight-man team that devised a multiphase plan for the economic development of Pakistan. Four years later, another Mason team put together a similar plan for Iran. A man of many parts and enormous energies, Mason was a member of the President's Committee to Strengthen the Security of the Free World, chairman of the Advisory Committee on Economic Development for AID, a consultant to the World Bank, and a consultant to numerous other agencies.

In organizing DAS, he recruited David Bell, from Truman's White House staff, and Gustav Papanek, formerly deputy director of program planning for Southeast Asia for AID. As its name implies, DAS provides teams of economic and political advisers for underdeveloped nations, for which it is paid by the government involved or by an American foundation. And considering the close ties that DAS staffers have had with various federal agencies, one might logically expect that the State Department has occasionally suggested to some friendly African or Asian government that it might be useful to ask for help and guidance from Harvard. Consequently, DAS has been asked to send advisory cadres to Argentina, Liberia, Iran, Indonesia, Malaysia, Ghana, Greece, Colombia and several other nations.

Papanek, for example, was director of a team that went to Ghana to advise the military junta which ousted the pro-socialist Kwame Nkrumah, and they were able to produce a detailed development plan less than a year after the coup. In fact, by September 1968, Papanek informed his colleagues at DAS, "The outlook for a successful project is good. The government is relatively stable, the top economic policymaker is competent, and the government is particularly receptive to foreign advisers."

But another DAS team, which was simultaneously advising the tottering Suharto regime in Indonesia, seemed somewhat less enthusiastic, as reflected in a confidential memo dated August 1968: "President Suharto continued to be influenced by the group of senior officers around him, many of them cronies from his earlier days but not otherwise distinguished either in terms of intellect or honesty.... Fortunately, a commitment of a larger amount of aid, and especially the substantial increases in PL 480 ["Food for Peace"] food grains helped to restore confidence."

As one can readily surmise, Harvard economists and the U.S. government have continued to act in tandem on development projects in various countries, often influenced by considerations that reflect the ideological aims of whatever administration happens to be in Washington.

## *The Russian Research Center*

Not long after Winston Churchill verbally erected the "Iron Curtain," a group of Harvard professors created the Russian Research Center. With funding from the Carnegie Corporation and the university itself, Clyde Kluckholn and several of his recently returned OSS colleagues began an in-depth study of all aspects of the Soviet Union, a field of academic inquiry that was instantly dubbed "the new Kremlinology." Actually, the original proposal for the center came not from Harvard but from John Gardner, then president of Carnegie and later secretary of HEW and even later chairman of Common Cause. No doubt influenced by a general concern about the cold war that began immediately after World War II, he suggested the development of a research program "upon those aspects of the field of Russian studies which lie peculiarly within the professional competence of social psychologists, sociologists and cultural anthropologists."

Expressing that aim in less formal terms, one of the center's younger researchers explained to his Radcliffe girlfriend, "We're just trying to psych out the commies."

A much more skeptical appraisal came from a graduate student in another department, who feared that the new center would lead to "the politicization of the social sciences" and to "the manipulation of research to suit the needs of the federal government's foreign policy."

In any event, the Russian Research Center's first major project was the "Refugee Interview Project," which sought to gain insights into the personalities of persons who had escaped from communist Eastern Europe, delving at length into specific grievances about social, economic, political and psychological conditions behind the Iron Curtain. Several scholars in the field later charged that some of the information gained from the interviews was used by U.S. intelligence agents for subsequent operations in that area.

Aside from such ad-hoc activities as the Refugee Interview Project, the center established a continuing but small Soviet Union Program for twenty graduate students a year. Although the program's initial orientation reflected the cold war policies of the Eisenhower-Kennedy-Johnson years, it shifted toward the détente views of Nixon and Kissinger in later years. One must presume that the center's present orientation is an admixture of Vance "moderation," Brzezinski "hard line," and Carter "confusion."

Among the center's most prominent researchers in its initial stages was Alex Inkeles, who guided his colleagues into large-scale gathering of information about Third World countries. A self-proclaimed leftist, Inkeles has worked on a number of studies that have been critical of the tough anti-communist line of conservative agencies like the State Department, which he considered ignorant of insurgent movements in Asia, Africa and Latin America. (As one of his fellow professors has observed, "Liberal social scientists like Inkeles are most useful to policy-makers who really want to understand insurgents: conservative scholars would deny or minimize the grievances of left-wing groups, while liberal scholars are perceptive and sympathetic.")

Nevertheless, one of his liberal detractors once charged that some of the center's research on Latin America could be used by reactionary counterinsurgents—to which Inkeles reportedly answered, "Our research is available to both sides."

## The East Asian Research Center

Another of Harvard's institutes, the East Asian Research Center, enjoys a reputation for impartiality and independence, and even in some circles for "pinkish" left criticism of government policy. More significant is the degree to which an institution priding itself for such independence can, with no attempt at concealment, cooperate with the U.S. government.

The Official Register of Harvard University, Vol. LXI, No. 16, states that EARC was founded in 1955 "with generous support from the Ford and Carnegie Foundations, as an agency to facilitate training and research of East Asia" because "the rise of a powerful and unfriendly Chinese state has been a new experience in American life, something not encompassed in earlier studies." The original generous support was soon supplemented by grants from the Department of Defense, the U.S. Air Force, and the U.S. Arms Control and Disarmament Agency.

The interchange of personnel is another badge of cooperation between Washington and EARC. Robert Bowie, mentioned elsewhere in this section, co-edited with John K. Fairbank one of EARC's earliest publications on Communist China, *China 1955-1959: Policy Documents with Analysis,* for a long time one of the basic texts for courses on the subject. The actual *author* of this work is unnamed, possibly for security reasons, but he evidently worked under the aegis of EARC. Morton Halperin enjoyed a joint appointment from the Center for International Affairs and EARC before moving to the Defense Department in 1967 and then to Henry Kissinger's White House staff. The chief attraction of EARC is Edwin O. Reischauer, ex-ambassador to Japan under President Kennedy and perhaps the most quoted "expert" on Asian foreign policy. Reischauer has long served as consultant to the government and is a virtual spokesman for both the U.S. and Japanese governments. The Department of State and other agencies regularly grant leave to their senior officials for study at EARC. These men are welcomed as "visiting scholars" doing normal research. In recent years the Central Intelligence Agency has "surfaced"—partly to improve its public image and partly to satisfy the intellectual aspirations of its researchers—and its personnel are present as special students and research associates. There is also the recent publication by Harvard University Press of an East Asian monograph by a CIA man, Charles Neuhauser, an analyst who also directed the EARC Red Guard Translation Project. Another CIA man, Sidney Bearman, was a visiting research fellow in 1968. (See *Harvard Crimson*, October 16 and 17, 1968.)

To prove its impartiality, however, the center claims to balance these years of collaboration with government agencies by sponsoring the visits of a French leftist (for a two-and-a-half-week stay) and of a Soviet scholar who is the Russian equivalent of a CIA researcher. However, when a pro-Communist Chinese tried to return to Harvard to finish Ph.D. work, he was not readmitted because it was feared his thesis would be "propaganda." EARC thus maintains both direct links and a basic political alignment with the U.S. foreign service.

### Harvard and National Defense

Like other major universities, Harvard has always participated in the nation's military efforts in wartime. "It should be a matter of record," wrote President Conant in his 1943-44 report, "that in the United States our educational institutions proved themselves to be so flexible and adaptable that they could render important assistance to the government in the prosecution of the war." Harvard's adaptability included some confidential instructional programs for army and navy personnel and two very large special laboratories engaged in secret work for the Office of Scientific Research and Development. Harvard professors were also deeply involved in the making of the atomic bomb.

When hot war against fascism became cold war against communism, Harvard's adaptable institutions continued to respond to the government's needs. In 1948 President Conant noted a "new, more intimate association" between Harvard and the federal government. This new relation, he wrote, "involves constant calls for the loan of the services of professors, contracts for all manner of research and scholarly undertakings with several different agencies." By 1951, he reported, "Numerous members of the university staff are heavily involved as consultants in highly confidential scientific matters connected with the armed forces. Indeed many professors here and elsewhere find themselves perplexed as to how to divide their time between calls from the government and their responsibilities as scholars and teachers." In the same year he disclosed that the business school was undertaking a "considerable" secret study for the Defense Department.

This involvement continued through the '50s. In 1968, for example, the university received $12,943,800 from the national defense establishment, broken down as follows:

| | |
|---|---|
| Atomic Energy Commission | $6,931,000 |
| Air Force | 966,800 |
| Army | 649,000 |
| Navy | 2,030,000 |
| Advanced Research Projects Agency | 1,237,000 |
| Arms Control and Disarmament Agency | 50,000 |
| Department of State | 1,060,000 |

But defense monies were only a fifth of all the government funding at Harvard (a total of $63,942,000 in fiscal year 1968). Next to the total defense budget, Harvard's share is infinitesimal. Nevertheless, it is significant and occasionally of real strategic importance. Most of the Pentagon money supposedly supports basic research, although the line between "basic" and "applied" research is, at best, thin.

The following lists of both military and nonmilitary projects provide some insight into the scope and breadth of the university's numerous contributions to U.S. and foreign research interests during the aforementioned period:

## Projects in and/or for Foreign Countries

*Country/Project Subject/Recipient/Date/Value*

Africa/Nutrition improvement/Harvard School of Public Health, F.J. Sture/ 5/20/68-6/30/68/ $2,000

Chile/Master tax reform program in Chile/ O. Oldman, Harvard Law School/ 7/1/66-9/30/69/ $393,500

China*/Motivational development of managers for industrial enterprises in China/ Center for Research and Pesonality/ 1967/ $17,850

Central America/Business management in Central America/ Harvard Business School/ 1967/ $947,380

Worldwide/Research study program relating to the importance of health in economic growth, oriented toward developing countries/ Harvard, Fellows/ 1967/ $85,756

Mexico/Project to transform traditional subsistence agricultural community into a modern organized production unit to produce for the market/ Harvard, Fellows/ 1967/ $264,342

*Sponsoring agency/Project title/Recipient/Date/Value*

Arabian-American Oil Co./Trachoma/Harvard School of Public Health/ 10/1/64-9/30/69/ $600,000

Corporation Venezolana de Guayana/Center in Ciudad Guayana/ Harvard Center for Studies in Education and Development/ 10/1/66-9/30/69/ $260,271.50

National Development Council of Argentina/Funding of Development Advisory Service/ 8/1/63-12/31/65/ $200,000

Pakistan Government/Economic Planning/Funding of Development Advisory Service/ 7/1/65-6/30/68/ $380,000

*Note that in State Department language "China" means Taiwan.

National Planning Agency of Liberia/Funding of Development Advisory Service/ 12/24/64–6/26/68/ $1,272,225

## U.S. Sponsored Research in Foreign Affairs

*Sponsoring Agency/Project title/Principal Researcher/Date/Value*

Air Force/Role of Third Parties in Conflict Resolution/ R.E. Walton Harvard Business School/ 9/5/68–6/30/69/ $35,000

Air Force/Military Implications of Change in China (to advance the state of knowledge in the field, to provide background for specialized studies and to provide the basis for projections)/ Lindbeck, Pelzel, Vogel, Clark, etc., East Asian Research Center/ 1967/ $176,000

Air Force/Communist China/Ezra Vogel, arts and sciences/ 1/1/64–6/30/68/ $363,500

Air Force/Classical Analysis/ L.V. Ahlfors, arts and sciences/ 1/1/65–5/31/69/ $356,500

Air Force/Socio-Cultural Aspects of Development/ Inkeles, arts and sciences/ 2/1/66–6/30/68/ $82,900

Arms Control and Disarmament Agency/Chinese Communist Doctrine and Practice Relating to International Law and Treaties/ J.A. Cohen, Harvard Law School/ 5/13/66–9/30/60/ $100,000

Central Intelligence Agency/Graphical Display and Extensible Languages in Text Manipulation Systems/ A.G. Oettinger, linguistics/ 7/1/68–7/1/69/ $25,000

Department of Defense/Proliferation Study/ Mid-East Regional Security and Possible Non-Proliferation/ Thomas C. Schelling/ 1967/ $32,400

Department of Health, Education and Welfare/Mexican Cultural Change/ Evon Vogt/ 1967/ $56,100

U.S. Navy/Group Processes under Different Conditions of Success and Failure/ D. Shapiro, Harvard Medical School/ 1967/ $27,000

U.S. Naval Academy/Evaluating Educational Systems/ L.M. Stolurow/ Harvard Graduate School of Education/ 12/1/67–6/30/68/ $127,500

Office of Internal Security Affairs/Strategic Analysis of Extralegal Internal Political Conflict/ T.C. Schelling, arts and sciences/ 9/1/66–8/31/69/ $256,600

Department of State/Formal Language in Behavioral Sciences/ G.A. Miller/ 6/27/63–6/30/69/ $650,000

Department of State/Computer Aided Teaching/ A.G. Miller/ 6/29/64-9/23/68/ $318,700

Department of State/Socio-Cultural Aspects of Development/ A. Inkeles, H. Schuman, arts and sciences/ 1/10/63-6/30/68/ $47,000

Department of State/Socio-Cultural Aspects of Development in India/ A. Inkeles, arts and sciences/ 5/24/63-6/30/68/ $38,000

Department of State/Ethiopian Orthodox Church and Ethiopian Society/ G.H. Williams, Harvard Divinity School/ 11/13/67-7/30/68/ $7,200

Department of State/Socio-Cultural Aspects of Development in Israel/ A. Inkeles, arts and sciences/ 6/17/63-6/30/68/ $63,000

Department of State/Industrial Entrepreneurship in Pakistan/ R. Vernon/ arts and sciences/ 11/9/64-3/31/68/ $7,500

Department of State/Study of the Military in China/ 1/1/63-11/14/67/ $76,100

## U.S. Sponsored Research in Chemical/Biological Warfare

*Sponsoring agency/Project title/Principal researcher/Value/Source*

U.S. Army, Edgewood Arsenal/"Membranes"/Dr. R.G. Spiro/ $60,000/ *Technical Abstract Bulletin*, 1968

U.S. Army, Edgewood Arsenal/Plant Samples Collected for Chemical Analysis (Colombia, Ecuador)/Leslie Gray and William Schopf/ Value unknown/*Technical Abstract Bulletin*, 1967 (There was another contract for another study of these plant samples undertaken by Dr. Djala D. Soljarto.)

U.S. Army, Edgewood Arsenal/Molecular Structure and Diffusional Processes Across Intact Epidermis/Dr. Robert J. Scheuplein/ $35,000/*Aerospace and Defense Research Contracts Roster*, 1965

U.S. Army, Edgewood Arsenal/Research to Determine the Structure of Puffer Poison (a highly toxic natural product as a model for new chemical agents)/Dr. R.B. Woodward/Value unknown/*Viet-Report*, Jan. 1968

U.S. Army, Fort Detrick/Laboratory Identification of BW Agents/Dr. Robert Fremont Smith/Value unknown/*Army Research Task Summary*, 1961 (This research aimed to "devise techniques and material for the rapid identification of BW agents and disease applicable to use in the Armed Forces.")

*Narcissism:* While the freedom, affluence and acceptability of America's single population represents significant changes in life-style and attitude, there are social critics who believe that the celebration of being single has dangers contained within it. David Riesman, professor of social sciences at Harvard, thinks that the trend to living alone is an expression of the new narcissism. "Something's missing and that is connectedness," he says. "Both sexes are more dependent than they admit. Jealousy is inadmissible and inevitable. We want fidelity. We want bonds—even though they may strangle us at times."

—"Going It Alone,"
Life/style, *Time* magazine

## CHAPTER VIII

**Harvard Social Scientists: Incestuous, Ubiquitous, Contentious**

IT HAS BEEN SAID that Harvard social scientists are incestuous, ubiquitous and extremely contentious—and there seems to be ample evidence to sustain all three charges.

According to the rather acerbic testimony of a prominent State University of New York sociologist, "These Harvard people are even more incestuous than the ruling clan of Saudi Arabia and about a thousand times more numerous." He preferred to remain anonymous "because they also tend to dominate the editorial boards of several academic journals that sometimes publish my articles," but he offered a detailed description of the gradual infiltration and ultimate takeover of the sociology department at the West Coast university where he received his doctoral degree and briefly taught:

"If you weren't from Cambridge, you couldn't possibly penetrate their inner circle, and they were constantly referring to their graduate work with Talcott Parsons, Erik Erikson, B.F. Skinner, David Riesman, Gordon Allport, Jerome Bruner, Pitirim Sorokin, Robert Bales, Jerome Kagan, Robert Coles and all the other Harvard big shots whose names dominate the reading lists of almost every college course in sociology, psychology and anthropology. So that after a while, you got the impression that Harvard was the only goddam university in the country."

Such sentiments, expressed with varying degrees of resentment (and occasional awe), are commonly heard in academic communities everywhere, particularly from graduates of Yale, Columbia, Stanford, the University of Chicago, USC, the University of California, MIT, Michigan University, Caltech, and other major universities—all of which have produced distinguished scholars and significant scholarly research.

If Harvard men are indeed incestuous (which seems obvious), it would logically follow that they are also ubiquitous, a fact easily discerned in a cursory review of scores of college catalogues. Several hundred serve on faculties in all fifty states, many of them functioning as department chairmen, deans and presidents. They can also be found in at least sixty-three foreign countries, where they are apt to be leaders of the academic elite— deservedly or not. As one Mexican intellectual recently commented, *"Carlos no es demasiado inteligente, pero su doctorado de Harvard le da ciertas ventajas"* ("Carlos is not excessively intelligent, but his doctorate from Harvard gives him certain advantages").

As for their being "contentious," one would have to say that the allegation is probably justified, but their contentiousness is internal as well as external. In fact, some of the intellectual squabbles within the Yard are as brutal as any family brawl over money or sex. During the '60s, when Professor Y and Professor Z were at swordpoint on the issue of ethnic studies, their children somehow persuaded them to declare a truce so that the two families could take a joint holiday on Martha's Vineyard. But hostilities were resumed on the very first night when Z refused to drink the wine Y had poured from a cut-glass decanter.

"You can't fool me with that fancy decanter," he said with a sneer. "That's Gallo wine and you're betraying Cesar Chavez!"

"If you can recognize it that easily," said Y, "you must drink a lot of it, chum."

Having thus accused each other of the most venal transgression, they studiously avoided each other for the rest of the holiday, communicating only through their wives, who had long before mutually agreed that they were married to a pair of "petulant little boys with high IQs."

In all fairness, one should note that most of the faculty's disputes are on a much more elevated plane. One of the most memorable controversies grew out of Professor B. F. Skinner's remarkable book *Beyond Freedom and Dignity*, which provoked a bitter debate that all but consumed the academic world in the fall of 1971.

Asserting that the time had come for man to surrender the individual rights he had always so fervently claimed, Skinner proposed a drastic redesign of modern culture so that mankind might survive. "To man *qua* man, we readily say good riddance," he wrote, coldly rejecting the existence of "autonomous man ... the man defended by the literature of freedom and dignity." As a substitute, Skinner envisaged a vast, all-pervasive institutional system with behavioral controls designed to encourage altruistic behavior and to eliminate less desirable "selfish behavior" such as overpopulation, war, pollution and crime. "We must delegate the control of the population as a whole to specialists—to police, priests, teachers, therapists and so on, with their specialized reinforcers and their codified contingencies."

As the world's foremost behavioral psychologist, Skinner had developed and "proved out" ingenious techniques for the radical modification of behavior—animal and human—employing what he called "operant conditioning." The so-called "teaching machine" and "programmed learning" were developed in his Harvard laboratory—and professionals on all six continents practiced his control devices upon thousands of patients, mental retardates, schizophrenics, homosexuals, convicts, soldiers, people living in communes, and ordinary schoolchildren. Skinner had tested his formulation of "operant behavior" with his legendary "Skinner box," in which he had created "a simple universe to reinforce, or shape, a specific behavior that could be observed and measured with precision." Having first taught pigeons how to peck at a lever that would cause food pellets to drop into the box, he eventually managed to teach the pigeons to play Ping-Pong.

"I'm frankly disappointed," remarked a Stanford psychologist when he heard about the experiment. "Since they're Harvard pigeons, you would expect them to learn how to play chess."

He was equally sarcastic about Skinner's contention that he knew precisely how people as well as pigeons learned—namely, through "operant conditioning," or the systematic use of rewards to encourage desired responses to specific stimuli.

"He's full of crap," said the Stanford professor. "But since he's at Harvard, a lot of people will take him seriously and will even ignore the fact that some people are a bit more complex than pigeons."

More bemused than distressed, a Denver University professor expressed the hope that his department chairman would hire a Skinner pigeon to act as his teaching assistant. "My freshman class is seriously overcrowded," he said. "And we could probably get one of those pigeons at a fairly low salary."

In a more serious vein, an increasing number of psychologists and social scientists had been extremely critical of the "sterility" and "omniscience" of behaviorism, so that Skinner's latest proposal was viewed as a prelude to the "Brave New World" of Aldous Huxley. One critic, Professor Richard L. Rubenstein, noted, "This utopian projection is less likely to be a blueprint for the Golden Age than for the theory and practice of hell." In *Psychology Today*, which devoted an entire issue (August 1971) to Skinner's challenging treatise, T. George Harris asserted, "His proposal now to redesign all of culture—government, education and economics—invokes a vision of the whole world as a Skinner box."

Emphasizing his long tenure at Harvard and once again

reinforcing the mystique of the university, *Time* magazine featured Skinner in its cover article for September 20, 1971, which referred to scores of newspaper editorialists and magazine writers who had given vent to grave reservations about the awesome and chilling implications of Skinner's "technology of behavior." When confronted by scholars, students and news reporters at the national convention of the American Psychological Association in Washington, D.C., the good-humored professor reminded them, "We're all controlled all the time. Parents control children and employers control employees—and they do it badly. We've got the means of controlling the human race right now, but we need to use them better." And when repeatedly asked who would devise and impose the behavioral controls, he somewhat defensively responded, "There isn't going to be any benevolent dictator—or there need not be one. The idea that regimentation necessarily follows cultural design is quite wrong. . . . But there is no other solution to [the world's] problems than the slow emergence of a new cultural pattern."

Paradoxically enough, Skinner has been a highly influential figure among American college students for almost three decades, mostly because of his utopian novel, *Walden Two*, which stressed many of the principles embodied in *Beyond Dignity and Freedom* and which has had a surprising increase in sales since it was published in 1948. The novel pictures a dream community where every man, woman and child has enough to satisfy basic needs, where all work is equally shared, where conspicuous consumption is forbidden and people learn never to want special rewards or honors—not even thank you's. But although his puritanical espousal of self-discipline and training is especially appealing to today's disillusioned youth, the sheer brilliance of Skinner's scholarship accounts for his broader and more sustained appeal to fellow social scientists. In a poll among academicians conducted by Southern Methodist University, he was the only living scholar to be ranked among the ten great minds in the history of psychology.

Some of his colleagues at Harvard are a bit less reverent. "He's had a lot of flash," says one of the younger psychologists. "But no sustained light."

"His pigeons will get bored playing Ping-Pong, and they'll eventually flee the coop," says another professor. "And so will Skinner's great reputation."

As for his students at Harvard, one of them once remarked, "He thinks in intriguing new paradoxes that are hard to accept—but even harder to ignore."

Less controversial than Skinner and perhaps more esteemed by his colleagues at Harvard and elsewhere, Erik Erikson has been a dominant force in various intellectual developments here and abroad. Dr. Peter Lomas, an eminent British scholar, has described him as "the most influential of living psychoanalysts," furthur stating, "In America he has no rival, and in Britain he is only challenged by Donald Winnicott."

His publications, which include more than a hundred books and articles, have been characterized by fellow humanist scholars as having had a pervasive influence not only on psychoanalysis but also on history, political science, religion, education, anthropology and the social sciences. In Dr. Lomas' estimation, Erikson has made at least four major contributions:

"First, his concept of 'identity' has emerged with sufficient power to impress itself upon the whole intellectual scene, linking several disciplines and disturbing sterile patterns of thought.

"Second, the concept of identity has helped psychoanalysis to come to terms with the fact that people are whole, unique beings and cannot be satisfactorily explained in terms of id, ego and superego.

"Third, in describing the vicissitudes of the sense of identity—in particular the identity crisis of adolescence—he had led the way to a new dimension of psychiatric thinking.

"Fourth, he has brought restraint upon the tendency to use psychoanalytical theory in a destructively moralistic way."

Born of Danish parents in 1902, Erikson spent most of his childhood and youth in Germany. Rather than studying at a university when he came of age, he spent several years wandering through Europe as a potential artist. Then, at the age of twenty-five, he accepted a friend's invitation to join Sigmund Freud's group in Vienna, where he was trained as a psychoanalyst. Migrating to the United States, he taught at Stanford, practiced for ten years at the Austen Riggs Center in Stockbridge, Massachusetts (1950–60), and was then appointed a professor at Harvard *without ever having received a college degree.* (Harvard provides an honorary M.A. to all permanent faculty members—so that every professor, whatever academic status he has achieved elsewhere, presumably enters the university on an equal footing.)

As Robert Coles puts it, "It is fair to say that in the middle and late '50s he became something more than a leading psychoanalyst; historians, theologians, philosophers and biologists took an increasing interest in his work, and so did students of all kinds—in colleges, in graduate schools, in medical schools, in the postgraduate programs to train interns and residents." He was invited to scores of meetings and lectured in universities throughout the United States and Europe. Meanwhile, he was writing at a furious pace. Two of his most-publicized books were collections of essays: *Insight and Responsibility* (1964) and *Identity: Youth and Crisis*, which became required reading on hundreds of campuses. In his previously published *Young Man Luther* and the celebrated, widely quoted monograph *Identity and the Life Cycle*, Erikson had essentially completed the basic structure of his thought, so that after 1958 he could "roamingly explore" the various ramifications of his primary beliefs and their application to a wide range of contemporary problems and issues: the relationship between politics and psychoanalysis; the emerging role of women; the socioeconomic aspects of race; the ever-confusing psychological development of young people; the emotional development of girls and young mothers; the role of religion in modern society; the ethical principles which underlie clinical and psychoanalytic work.

In 1953, Erikson was invited to a meeting of the World Health Organization in Geneva, where twelve leading scientists engaged in several momentous discussions on "the influences of biological, psychological and cultural factors in the development through childhood of the adult personality." Among the participants were Konrad Lorenz, Margaret Mead, Jean Piaget, John Bowlby and Julian Huxley. Commenting on Erikson's contributions, which figured prominently in two of the four volumes that ultimately resulted from the meeting, Huxley wrote: "I was very much interested in Erikson's chart. We may disagree with this or that detail, but we now have a comprehensive statement of the method of psychobiological development and the possibility of its continuity. It is not uniform but epigenetic, as he rightly said, in that novelty arises during the process...."

The chart to which Huxley refers, reproduced here, illustrates what Erikson called "the life cycle." It has been carefully studied, memorized and reproduced by thousands of professors and students, who have come to regard its neat formulation as the very essence of psychological truth. Keenly aware that most people crave the appearance of order and that literal-minded students would see the chart as a ready explanation for all kinds of psychological problems, Erikson has repeatedly cautioned that it "is only a tool to think with, and cannot aspire to be a prescription to abide by, whether in the practice of child-training, in psychotherapy, or in the methodology of child study."

But in spite of Erikson's warning, thousands of students have been instantly seduced by the visual precision of his chart, often reciting the eight stages of the life cycle as if they are commandments deeply engraved on the human psyche. As one skeptic remarked, "Some people regard him as the new Moses of Harvard, from where all wisdom supposedly emanates." He went on to say, "There is a mystique about Erik Erikson which, when combined with the Harvard mystique, has increased by geometric progression."

| | 1 | 2 | 3 | 4 | 5 | 6 | 7 | 8 |
|---|---|---|---|---|---|---|---|---|
| VIII Maturity | | | | | | | | Ego integrity vs. Despair |
| VII Adulthood | | | | | | | Generativity vs. Stagnation | |
| VI Young adulthood | | | | | | Intimacy vs. Isolation | | |
| V Puberty and adolescence | | | | | Identity vs. Role confusion | | | |
| IV Latency | | | | Industry vs. Inferiority | | | | |
| III Locomotor-genital | | | Initiative vs. Guilt | | | | | |
| II Muscular-anal | | Autonomy vs. Shame, Doubt | | | | | | |
| I Oral sensory | Basic trust vs. Mistrust | | | | | | | |

Less well known to the general public than either Skinner or Erikson is a man who has achieved an almost immortal status among social scientists—Talcott Parsons. Although none of his many books have been best sellers or the subjects of cover articles in popular magazines, both his disciples and detractors probably would agree that no other living sociologist has had more impact on modern social thought and theory than Parsons. When discussing his work, sociologists talk not about "Parsons' theories" but about "Parsonian theory," just as most scholars refer to two other landmarks in human thought as Darwinian theory and Copernican theory.

In the words of Robert Reinhold, "Even younger sociologists, many of whom sharply differ with him about sociology, accord him a religious-like reverence before going on to do things in their own fashion, much the way Italian Catholics genuflect before the Pope and then vote Communist." Putting it more succinctly, one of his former students said, "Everybody has got to kneel and make the sign of the cross before him, for Talcott Parsons is a god—but it's still okay to take a potshot at him."

The substance of Parsonian theory is so complex and abstract that only a few professional sociologists claim to understand it completely; but it seems to rest on the premise that all human societies, whether simple or complex, share the same basic organizing principles. Called "structural functionalism," the theory holds that all social phenomena have a necessary function in holding society together and that societies have an overall structure that governs the interactions of its members. Thus, a society is basically a system which operates on many different levels, with each of its parts interdependent on the others, so that a change in one elicits a corresponding reaction in the other parts. Parsons also likens the social system to the biological system, wherein all organisms are in equilibrium with their environment and with each other.

And like biological systems, says Parsons, social systems have "regulatory mechanisms that allow them to return to equilibrium after each disturbance." Consequently, even as conflicting forces are temporarily disrupting the body of the system, the mechanisms of social control tend to keep the system as a whole in "dynamic equilibrium." It is this particular aspect of Parsonian theory that younger sociologists consider politically conservative because "it stresses the tendency of societies to resist change by re-equilibrating themselves."

Among the principal cornerstones of his societal theorem is what Parsons calls the "four-function paradigm," according to which a society's structure is governed by the way it meets four basic needs: (1) "goal attainment," or the methods by which a system mobilizes to achieve its goals; (2) "adaptation," or its adjustment to the environment for survival; (3) "integration," or the internal relations of the system's various units, designed to reconcile conflicts and maintain cohesion; and (4) "pattern maintenance," the means by which a system deals with pressures to deviate from accepted norms.

Needless to say, these are oversimplifications of the vast and complex theoretical structures devised by Parsons during his forty-two years on the Harvard faculty, where he was a giant among giants. On his retirement at the age of seventy in 1973, more than 150 of his past and present students and colleagues converged on Cambridge to honor him at a testimonial dinner, which resulted in a seven-column article in *The New York Times*. Ranging in age from twenty-three to sixty-three, they came from universities in almost every state in the union and from several foreign countries, including Germany, India, France and Mexico, suggesting the scope of his influence in both time and space.

"Here it is," said one of the younger guests, glancing around the banquet hall, "the real intellectual mafia—and Talcott is our godfather."

'Well, he's only *one* of the godfathers," said an older colleague. "You've got Skinner and Erikson and Bruner and Riesman and whoever—each one with his own mafia."

If one accepts that metaphor, Harvard would be the academic Sicily, with each of its various departments headed by a godfather or several godfathers with separate little mafias representing his or her speciality within a given department—all much-touted scholars who have been described as "the greatest living———," a designation too frequently used by journalists but which is sometimes fairly accurate.

In the field of infant and early childhood development, Professor Jerome Bruner is truly among the greatest living scholars and is often described as the Jean Piaget of America. Until recently the director of Harvard's Center for Cognitive Studies, this sixty-two-year-old psychologist is now teaching at Oxford, where he continues to explore the intricate and complex processes by which an infant learns to think and to communicate.

Through countless experiments and imaginative theoretical formulations, Bruner has convincingly demonstrated that early childhood is the most critical period for learning—that our most important cognitive development occurs before the age of seven, about 50% of it before the age of four and the most basic aspects in the first eighteen months. His findings, many of which appeared in *A Study of Thinking* (1956) and *The Process of Education* (1960), have profoundly influenced educational policies all over the world, often provoking amazement or wrath among traditionalists who almost automatically resist new ideas. Indeed, some of his detractors have made snide comments about the games and toylike apparatus in the laboratory of his center, where infants and toddlers had for many years engaged in seemingly playful tests with the ever-smiling avuncular professor as he sought to prove or disprove his latest hypothesis about human understanding.

At the 21st International Congress of Psychology in Paris, Bruner took issue with the popular notion that infants are born "egocentric" and that their acquisition of language is accomplished through some innate skill. "If you look at the child's behavior as he develops procedures of communication," said Bruner, "you cannot help but be struck by the fact that from the start the child is sociocentric. The child communicates not only because it is alive but because it is stressful for the child to be in a noncommunicative situation."

But, according to Bruner, learning to talk is no sudden discovery. Indeed, it generally takes about two years of persistent effort and constant practice—by the mother as well as the infant. The mentor need not be the child's natural mother but may be a "vicar" from the adult community in which the infant lives. In any event, every word the vicar uses is "a lesson" in what sounds and tones function best in communicating the child's needs or intentions. Within a short time the baby's noises already show certain patterns: a cry followed by a pause to listen for reactions, then another cry. Thus, by the age of two months the child has learned to make cries that "demand" or simply "request"—that also express hunger, discomfort and fear. "Mother talk" corresponding to "baby talk" lets the child know that its request will be met, letting him know the consequences of his different types of cries.

Consequently, says Bruner, "Linguistic competence is developing before language proper." But in addition to making sounds, the parent and child use their eyes to communicate. In fact, the mother usually spends much of the first few months simply trying to discover what the child is looking at. By the age of four months, according to Bruner, 20% of babies can be induced to follow their mother's gaze; and that figure increases to 40% for children one year old—even when the mother is looking at an object behind the baby. Meanwhile, from about the age of ten months, the child begins learning the names of objects even though it may not be able to pronounce the names, and it does so through a three-step process: (1) mother points to an object; (2) mother asks, "what—or who or where—is that?"; and (3) she then labels the object, person or place: "That's a chair," "That's daddy," "That's the kitchen."

Thus, without knowing it, the mother has initiated the age-old and fundamental process of fostering the four basic skills that Bruner deems essential in later language development:

1. "Well-formedness," when the mother demands a closer approximation to the correct pronunciation of a word with each repetition (which means that the child will adopt the mother's notion of the "correct" pronunciation, whether or not it actually is).

2. "Truth functionality," generally begun after the first year, when mother corrects a mistake ("That's *not* a dog, it's a cat").

3. "Felicity," which means that the manner of speech must be appropriate to the situation—or what the mother customarily considers "appropriate" in said situation.

4. "Versimilitude," when the mother allows the child to place

a box on its head and pretends the box is a hat, but does not encourage the child to do the same thing with a less likely object such as a ball.

Commenting on this step-by-step, gradual accretion of words and meanings, Bruner has said, "Man realizes his full heritage when he reaches language. But he is learning things along the way which are also remarkable."

His own language is occasionally awkward and fuzzy, sometimes creating the impression that he's groping for a clearer definition of his own theories or that he's searching for new meanings in old words. To one of his ardent supporters Bruner's occasional linguistic imprecision simply means that "Jerry's ideas are sometimes too complex, too profound for ordinary conventional language."

"That's a lotta crap—Harvard crap!" says an irate UCLA professor. "If Bruner were teaching anywhere else, people would see that some of his stuff is either obtuse or too damned simplistic."

As previously noted herein, this often-bitter resentment of Harvard is constant and all-pervasive in academic circles, and it periodically prompts accusations that are clearly erroneous. Recently, for example, someone remarked that David Riesman's *The Lonely Crowd* was "just another slice of baloney from Harvard"—although the book was written while Riesman was teaching at Yale and published after he had joined the faculty at the University of Chicago (several years before he went to Cambridge). But even after his error had been pointed out, the man refused to budge from his initial opinion: "Well, he got his basic ideas for the book while getting his Ph.D. in sociology at Harvard—and it's still baloney."

Actually, Riesman majored in chemistry at Harvard as an undergraduate, then switched to the law school, where his high grade average earned him a clerkship with Justice Brandeis of the U.S. Supreme Court. Thereafter, he taught law at the University of Rochester, but his insatiable curiosity about all human problems eventually led him into the social sciences—which in turn resulted in his writing *The Lonely Crowd: A Study of the Changing American Character** (1950), *Faces in the Crowd* (1952), *Individualism Reconsidered* (1954) and numerous other articles and books since then.

In what seemed like oversimplification to some of his fellow social scientists, Riesman declared that modern civilization had produced three types of human personalities, who were "tradition-directed, inner-directed, or other-directed." The three types were carefully delineated in *The Lonely Crowd*, which one reviewer described as a "typological menagerie," adding, "The occupants of the cages are not real people, who are almost always a blend of a blend of types. But real people and real politics can be understood better by walking through Riesman's zoo, reading the signs on the cages and looking at the occupants."

"Tradition-directed" man, according to Riesman, was formed in societies where there is minimal technological change or population growth, where each generation lives the kind of life that existed in previous generations, with sons carefully imitating their fathers. For example, most of Asia has been tradition-directed—and so was all of Europe before the Renaissance–Reformation period. But with its technological progress, population growth and the replacement of the feudal system with more fluid social patterns, Western Europe moved into a new phase where tradition-directedness was no longer viable.

"Inner-directed" man, said Riesman, was the inevitable outgrowth of a new society geared to mass production. Ever-increasing and fluid populations created mounting consumer demands that could be best satisfied by a new breed of man—the inner-directed man, who was "inventive, hard-working, willing to take risks and goal-oriented," characteristics developed with the aid of "inner gyroscopes" that enabled him to determine his

*Written with Reuel Denney and Nathan Glazer.

personal goals at an early age. But there came a time—roughly
fixed by Riesman as about 1920 for the United States—when
certain social and economic changes caused a shift in emphasis
from production to consumption, from "the hard struggle with
the material world to an easier existence centered around
relations with other people." Employment declined in mining,
farming and even manufacturing, while it rose in the service
trades, thus creating a new array of consumer demands.

"Other-directed" man now became a principal ingredient of
modern society. "What is common to all other-directed men,"
said Riesman, "is that their contemporaries are the source of
direction for the individual—either those known to him or those
with whom he is indirectly acquainted, through friends and
through the mass media. This source is, of course, 'internalized'
in the sense that dependence on it for guidance in life is implanted
early. The goals toward which the other-directed person thrives
shift with that guidance; it is only the process of striving itself
and the process of paying close attention to signals from others
that remain unaltered through life."

In Riesman's estimation, the working-class American is
largely inner-directed; and the old middle class—farmers, small
businessmen, bankers, technically minded engineers—is still
lagely inner-directed. But the new middle class—bureaucrats,
salaried business employees, etc.—is predominantly other-directed. Spreading in numbers and influence, other-directed people
are more prominent in New York than in Boston, in Los Angeles
than in Spokane, in Cincinnati that in Chillicothe.

*Sociability* is the key factor for other-directed persons, and this
is reflected in the schooling and raising of youngsters. As
Riesman says, "The children are supposed to learn democracy
by underplaying the skills of intellect and overplaying the skills
of gregariousness and amiability—skill democracy, in fact, based
on ability to do something, tends to survive only in athletics."
Consequently, such children are doggedly amiable and are often
incapable of strong emotion or deep love. "They will be

compulsively gregarious—and lonely. Their play will be deadened by anxious groupiness." To illustrate this point, he cited the following bit of dialogue with a twelve-year-old girl:

*A:* I like Superman better than the others because they can't do everything that Superman can do. Batman can't fly, and that is very important.
*Q:* Would you like to be able to fly?
*A:* I would like to be able to fly if everybody else did, but otherwise it would be too conspicuous.

In a lengthy cover article on Riesman in *Time* magazine (Sept. 27, 1954), one critic said, "His books cut across the social sciences, picking a method of treatment out of anthropology and using it to handle a political exposition. He can mingle ideas from psychoanalysis and economics and enrich the result with literary references from Tolstoy, Samuel Butler, Virginia Woolf, Castiglione, Jules Verne, Franz Kafka, St. Augustine, Nietzsche, E. M. Forster, Lionel Trilling, Cervantes, Jack London and James Joyce. His books are relatively free of academic jargon, because there is no special idiom that the economists, social scientists and anthropologists have in common; anyone who wants to talk to all of them has to use English."

But professors who write best sellers and become subjects of cover articles in magazines like *Time* are often deemed suspect in the upper reaches of academia, particularly in places such as Harvard, where popular approval is apt to be disdained as evidence of shallow scholarship. As one might expect, some of Riesman's colleagues have occasionally expressed a hint of disdain with respect to his "public successes," though most of his peers seem to accept him as an equal.

Among the less celebrated but highly respected social scientists are Robert Freed Bales, H. Stuart Hughes, and Jerome Kagan, each of whom has made significant contributions in his special area. Director of the Laboratory for Social Relations since 1969, Bales collaborated with Talcott Parsons in writing *Working*

*Papers in the Theory of Action* (1953) and *Family, Socialization and Interaction Process* (1955). He has also written and lectured at several major universities on the relationship between alcoholism, ethnicity and social class. Hughes has written a three-volume survey of European social thought—*Consciousness and Society* (1958), *The Obstructed Path* (1968) and *The Sea Change* (1975)—which was quite favorably reviewed in various journals.

Aside from the contributions of its immediate faculty, the university has spread its influence far beyond Cambridge through hundreds of graduates, some of whom have achieved distinction of a singular nature.

Paul Gebhardt, for example, collaborated with Alfred Kinsey in researching and writing their landmark study *The Sexual Behavior of the American Female:* and he is now director of the famous Kinsey Institute for the Study of Sexual Behavior. (One of his former classmates recently remarked, "Paul had to learn all about sex in order to get over his innate shyness.")

Stanley Milgram, an apt student of B. F. Skinner's behavioral concepts, created a national furor with his 1963 experiment on "obedience to authority," in which a group of his Yale students obediently followed instructions to administer electrical shocks of increasing intensity to an errant "learner" each time he gave a wrong answer. Although it was a fake test, with the "learner" merely pretending to suffer acute anguish, Milgram was strongly criticized in *American Psychologist* for being "unforgivably unethical." Others praised his ingenuity.

In a wide-ranging article on Milgram's work for *Psychology Today* (June 1974), Carol Travis delved into his academic background in considerable detail:

Milgram applied to Harvard and sent along a lengthy application letter, which he read to me. "I view man not as an isolated psychological entity," he wrote, "but as an adaptive organism living in association with and reacting to his fellow men." This view pervades Milgram's subsequent work, especially that on obedience and life in cities. "My application letter was very prescient, even though I thought it was a lot of baloney at the time."

Harvard must have thought it was baloney too, because it rejected him. Disappointed but undaunted, Milgram wrote another letter, volunteering to make up his deficiencies in psychology. Whereupon, he was admitted as a special student. From Harvard Milgram went to Yale as an assistant professor, and began his studies of obedience to authority. He stayed at Yale for three years and then returned to Harvard's Department of Social Relations, where he developed many imaginative approaches to the study of real-life social questions, such as the "lost-letter technique and the small-world problem." [In 1967 he moved to his current position as professor of psychology at the Graduate Center of the City University of New York.]

Another highly publicized graduate—whose notoriety has proved less beneficial—is Dr. Timothy Leary, a former psychology lecturer at Harvard, who used some of his undergraduate students in LSD experiments. Once the subject of innumerable newspaper and magazine articles, Leary was seldom mentioned without some reference to his Harvard past. Many of these articles said that Leary had been fired from the Harvard faculty.

But as Professor Bales correctly reports, "We didn't fire Leary. We simply decided not to renew his contract."

Harvard professors—even the most eminent ones—are not always absorbed in intellectual pursuits. Like professors all over the world, they occasionally indulge in the most ancient pursuit—sexual gratification.

According to several department secretaries, one of the nation's most honored psychologists has been a compulsive fanny pincher for years. He also stares at almost any woman who comes within his range of vision, studiously appraising her physical attributes as if she were one of the birds he studies in his laboratory. But in spite of his great reputation and celebrity status, his success with females is apparently not overwhelming.

"He always smells like those birds he experiments with," said one secretary. "And he never brushes the feathers off of his sloppy clothes."

In a somewhat similar vein, a young lab technician in the biology department has resisted the amorous advances of her middle-aged professor boss "because he always smells like formaldehyde."

Perhaps the most graphic example of professorial hanky-panky is the case of Professor X, a distinguished social scientist, who was known as "the lunger" to the wives of younger faculty members. On one memorable occasion, Professor X was one of several dinner guests at the apartment of one of his protégés. During the final stages of the meal, he wandered into the kitchen, where the young and very pretty hostess was preparing coffee— then suddenly there was a loud crash and banging as Professor X lunged for her with a sudden passion, causing several pots and pans to come tumbling off a shelf.

"I was helping her put away the pans," he explained rather sheepishly when some of the guests rushed toward the kitchen. "But you know how clumsy I am."

"Yes, we all know *very well* how clumsy you are," said his wife.

Besides, I didn't shout when I talked, she added, which was the way she remembered the Science graduates at Harvard. None of her classmates at Radcliffe had dated any boys from Science; they were déclassé.

Shortly before leaving, I ran into Lawrence Erbst, one of the four or five members of the class to proceed from Science to Harvard. I asked him if it had been true that Science grads had been marked apart at Harvard, if he had felt separate and declasse. He began to bristle angrily. At 16, he had been short and pugnacious, smart and witty, his voice something like a cross between a bark and a rasp. . . .

Now, clad in a neat gray suit, a lawyer, Harvard-educated with a degree from Harvard Law School, he looked exactly the way he had at school. Only his hair had become even more prominent, for it had turned a clear, pure white.

That was nonsense, he exclaimed. The kids from Science mingled with everyone. Whoever told me that didn't know what she was talking about. His voice grew louder. The Science grads were indistinguishable from everyone else at Harvard. He fumed. It had been a great school. Harvard. And Science. Science and Harvard. That, after all, was the dream come true. Merit ruling all.

—Gene Lichtenstein,
"The Great Bronx Science
Dream Machine," *The New York Times*

# CHAPTER IX The Graduate School of Education: Focus of Racial Controversy

SEVERAL YEARS AGO, at a cocktail party in Cambridge, one of the guests was relaying a bit of gossip about a neighbor's extremely active sex life. "Lulu is a kooky but very attractive astrologist," she said to several very attentive listeners. "And her former lovers have run the gamut from plumbers to undertakers—but now she's having this torrid affair with a Harvard professor, so Lulu is really moving up in the world."

"Well," said the informant's husband with a deprecatory smile, "he's merely a professor at the school of education—so she's not necessarily *moving up.*"

The other guests laughed knowingly at his *bon mot*, as if his put-down had expressed an accepted truth—and, indeed, almost everyone in Cambridge feels that the Harvard Graduate School of Education is at the very bottom of the university's totem pole. Even its faculty and most of the students are aware (often painfully, defensively aware) of their lowly status within the academic community. This is true, of course, in universities throughout the country. But in the caste-conscious ambience of

[163]

Harvard, such inferiority complexes are perhaps more deeply felt, more apt to produce compensatory syndromes. For example, persons who get doctoral degrees from the "ed school" are apt to insist on being addressed as "Doctor" X; whereas the alumni of the more prestigious branches of Harvard are apt to deemphasize or ignore their doctoral titles. In this regard, it should be noted that the school of education cannot confer a Ph.D. (Doctor of Philosophy) but is restricted to conferring an Ed.D. (Doctorate in Education), the university having obviously judged its intellectual level as somewhat lower than its other graduate schools—except for the business school, which confers only a master's degree.

But its inferior rank within the Harvard community is contradicted by the eminence of the ed school outside Cambridge. Indeed, its faculty and graduates have had an incalculable influence on educational practices and policies throughout the United States and numerous foreign countries, although certain educators feel that it is sometimes more negative than positive.

Particularly significant is Harvard's deep and continuing involvement in what has been called "the single most influential educational institution in the world"—*Sesame Street*. First of all, one must realize that *Sesame Street* reaches more children than any other medium, and that it reaches them at a most critical age, profoundly affecting their intellectual processes and their social attitudes. In fact, this much-celebrated television show has been "the first exposure to formal learning" for millions of three-to-six-year-old children in this country and many more millions in fifty-two foreign countries.

What they learn—and how they learn it—has been determined by a group of specialists in early-childhood education, an advisory board carefully selected from several universities and school systems; but the basic core of this board was a group of professors from the Harvard Graduate School of Education. One member of this advisory board (a professor from a rival university) once referred to the Cambridge contingent as "the Harvard mafia." However one may choose to characterize them, individually or collectively, one cannot overestimate the influence of Professors Jean Chall, Courtney Cazden, Helen Pope and—most particularly—Gerald Lesser, whose individual and joint contributions have become an integral part of the *Sesame Street* curriculum. As chairman of the advisory board and member of the board of trustees of the Children's Television Workshop, Lesser has been a principal moving force in every major production of CTW. Brilliant, innovative and possessed of apparently inexhaustible energy, he has skillfully bridged the gap between academia and the highly professional television producers at CTW, all ably led by Joan Ganz Cooney, the creator of *Sesame Street* and president of the parent organization.

As if to tighten the bond between Harvard and *Sesame Street*, one of CTW's top producers Sam Gibbon spent a year at the ed school, sharpening his already keen sense of the cognitive processes of children. And in a reciprocal exchange of ideas, executive producer David Connell has periodically commuted to Cambridge to teach a seminar on production techniques.

Regarding the financial aspect of *Sesame Street*, one should note that its initial multimillion-dollar support came from the Ford Foundation, the Carnegie Foundation and the U.S. Office of Education, all of which were headed by Harvard men— McGeorge Bundy, Alan Pifer and Harold Howe. Alluding to this fortuitous circumstance at a dinner-dance celebrating the tenth anniversary of the workshop, Howe remarked, "I'm happy to say that the old-boy network very wisely supported Joan Cooney's magnificent project."

But, in spite of its apparent stamp of approval from Harvard, *Sesame Street* has not been free of criticism. In their widely quoted book *Remote Control: Television and the Manipulation of American Life*, Frank Mankiewicz and Joel Swerdlow express certain misgivings about the long-range effects of this daily program:

Many teachers began to focus on the undeniable fact that learning from *Sesame Street* is by definition passive. Good educators believe that learning must be more than a spectator sport, and that if we have learned anything over the painful progress of teacher training since the early days of John Dewey, it is that the child must be involved in the learning process. Even the most conservative critics of modern primary education would not return to the days of a century ago when children sat quietly for hours while teachers lectured. But television—including *Sesame Street*—may have already accomplished that reversion.

It is one thing for a cartoon character to reveal with comic emphasis that 3 plus 2 equals 5, and quite another for the child to struggle with the concept himself—perhaps with Cuisinier rods—to reach the same solution. Many teachers use films, Jean Piaget wrote in 1969, because they mistakenly believe that "the mere fact of perceiving the objects and their transformations will be equivalent to direct action of the learner in the experience." This is a "grave error," Piaget explained, because "action is only instructive when it involves the spontaneous participation of the child himself, with all the tentative gropings and apparent waste of time such involvement implies."

The producers of *Sesame Street* are highly qualified professionals who are well aware that this participation problem exists. But they are bound by the need to attract children to sit down voluntarily in front of a television set—and that by definition creates passive viewers. Indeed, it is CTW's success in attracting and keeping an audience of children which makes the program a success—and CTW knows it. Thus *Sesame Street* not only does *not* encourage children to learn through some sort of individual struggle, but it is designed to give the child the impression that the program will not require any effort that could be even remotely unpleasant. The only concessions to the need for participation are cosmetic, such as the decision not to let the adult characters on the program adopt a child character, because viewers would feel jealous and lose their sense of participation. One might well ask, "What sense?"

Commenting on the passivity induced by television watching, Bruno Bettelheim wrote in 1960, "My concern is less with the content and much more with what persistent watching does to a child's ability to relate to real people, to become self-activated, to think on the basis of his own life experience instead of in stereotypes out of shows.... The emotional isolation from others that starts in front of television may continue in school. Eventually it leads, if not to a permanent instability, then to a reluctance to becoming active in learning or in relation to other people."

An additional concern of Mankiewicz and other critics is that *Sesame Street* watchers are not permitted to figure out whether there may be more than one answer to a given question. "Frequently, the program does not even allow itself time to provide an explanation," they say, so that children may be learning to give correct answers in response to specific but irrelevant cues. Thus, "the child watching *Sesame Street* knows these cues will be visible and entertaining, and that if he does not use them to pursue the correct answer, he can sit back with the calm confidence—always justified—that it will be forthcoming anyway, also in an entertaining way. The children are thus totally shielded from the need to master deduction, a process that may be more important than the correct answers to *any* set of questions."

Acknowledging that constant "box watching" does induce passivity, Lesser and his colleagues at Harvard and CTW constantly remind the critics that American children were already unfortunately addicted to television *before* the advent of *Sesame Street*; and that *Sesame Street* and its companion show, *Electric Company*, are much more stimulating and educationally helpful than other children's shows. Moreover, according to in-depth studies of audience reactions, both productions often encourage an intellectual and emotional participation by their young viewers.

Assessing the value of *Sesame Street*, anthropologist Margaret Mead has characterized it as "the most important program that has ever been developed for children as a way of introducing them to some of the basic tools necessary for the attainment of literacy." Her views are echoed by John Mathews, the highly regarded education writer for the Washington *Star*, who says, "There is no doubt that *Sesame Street* has had a greater impact on how and what preschool children learn and think than virtually any other teaching tool in this century." (One should note that it is the most honored show in television history, having received more than a hundred awards, including ten Emmys, one Peabody, the Prix Jeunesse in France, and the Japan Prize.)

But in the eyes of a Marxist professor in New York, "such honors merely indicate that the show pleases the Establishment— that it promotes white middle-class values in ethnic garb. But what would you expect of a show so heavily influenced by Harvard, the very heart of the Establishment?"

Harvard's involvement in *Sesame Street* has been relatively free of controversy, but this cannot be said of the ed school's major publication, the *Harvard Educational Review*—which, to the delight of female students, is often referred to as *HER*. Unlike most academic journals, which are seldom noticed by the general public, *HER* has been the focus of at least three extremely bitter controversies that ultimately led to significant changes in governmental policies and in the attitudes of thousands of teachers.

The most heated dispute—certainly the most publicized—was ignited by *HER's* publication in 1969 of an article titled "How Much Can We Boost IQ and Scholastic Achievement" by Professor Arthur Jensen. Ultimately concluding that inferior genes were a principal cause of low IQ-test scores of black children, Jensen began his article with the flat assertion that compensatory education efforts had failed to produce lasting effects on children's IQ and scholastic achievement. He then questioned the central premise upon which Head Start and other similar programs had been based: that IQ differences were almost entirely a result of environmental differences and the cultural bias of IQ tests.

Having defined the concept of intelligence and related it to other forms of mental ability, Jensen used an "analysis of variance" model to explain how IQ might be separated into genetic and environmental components. He then discussed his concept of "heritability," a statistical tool which supposedly assessed the degree to which individual differences in a trait like intelligence could be accounted for by genetic factors. He then offered "several lines of evidence" which presumably suggested that the heritability of intelligence is quite high (i.e., that genetic factors are much more important than environmental factors in producing IQ differences).

Jensen then proceeded to analyze the environmental influences that might be the most critical in determining IQ and concluded that *prenatal conditions* were perhaps the most significant environmental influence. Nevertheless, he still contended that social class and racial variations in IQ could not be accounted for by environmental differences but must be attributed to genetic differences. Then, after a detailed review of the results of several compensatory education programs for young children, he concluded that the changes in IQ produced by such programs were "generally small." He further stated that environment merely acts as a "threshold variable" with respect to intrinsic intelligence—that extreme environmental deprivation can keep the child from performing up to his genetic potential, but an enriched educational program cannot push the child above that fixed potential. As for so-called "diverse levels of intelligence between racial groups," one should note the specific passages of Jensen's provocative article:

*Negro Intelligence and Scholastic performance.* Negroes in the United States are disproportionately represented among groups identified as culturally or educationally disadvantaged. This, plus the fact that Negroes constitute by far the largest racial minority in the United States, has for many years focused attention on Negro intelligence. It is a subject with a now vast literature which has been quite recently reviewed by Dreger and Miller (1960, 1968) and by Shuey (1966), whose 578 page review is the most comprehensive, covering 382 studies. The basic data are well known: on the average, Negroes test about 1 standard deviation (15 IQ points) below the average of the white population in IQ, and this finding is fairly uniform across the 81 different tests of intellectual ability used in the studies reviewed by Shuey.

There is an increasing realization among students of the psychology of the disadvantaged that the discrepancy in their average performance cannot be completely or directly attributed to discrimination or inequalities in education. It seems not unreasonable, in view of the fact that intelligence variation has a large genetic component, to hypothesize that genetic factors may play a part in this picture. But such an hypothesis is anathema to many social scientists. The idea that the lower average intelligence and scholastic performance of Negroes could involve, not only environmental, but also genetic, factors had indeed been strongly denounced (e.g., Pettigrew, 1964). But it has been neither contradicted nor discredited by evidence....

As one might have expected, Jensen's article produced violent reactions from coast to coast. Scores of educators, public officials and black leaders denounced his theories as "racist, pernicious and false." And many of the critics bitterly assailed *HER* and Harvard in general for "allowing Jensen to use the university as a platform for racist ideology." One prominent black scholar, no doubt voicing the sentiment of most of his colleagues, accused the editors of *HER* of irresponsible behavior. "Surely, they must realize," he said, "that the general public will accept this vicious nonsense as gospel truth simply because it has been published in a Harvard journal. They have, in fact, given Jensen the stamp of approval of a great university, and they cannot justify their lack of moral responsibility by saying it's academic freedom."

In much the same vein, a white Catholic priest sadly remarked, "Harvard has helped Jensen stigmatize our entire black population, has given the bigots an intellectual excuse for racism."

In a more direct refutation of Jensen's thesis, Professor I. I. Gottesman, a leading behavioral geneticist, noted, "...even when gene pools are known to be matched, appreciable differences in mean IQ can be observed that could only have been associated with environmental differences." In his study of thirty-eight pairs of identical twins reared in *different environ-*

*ments,* the average variation in IQ for these identical twins was 14 points, and at least one-quarter of these pairs of twins had differences in IQ *that were larger than 16 points,* which was larger than the average difference between black and white populations. All of which let Gottesman to conclude, "The difference observed so far between whites and Negroes can hardly be accepted as sufficient evidence that with respect to intelligence the Negro American is genetically less endowed."

Harvard's Jerome S. Kagan, one of the nation's most distinguished developmental psychologists, fully supported Gottesman's criticism:

Let us consider some additional empirical evidence that casts doubt on the validity of Jensen's position. Longitudinal studies being conducted in our laboratory reveal that lower class white children perform less well than middle class children on tests related to those used in intelligence tests. These class differences with white populations occur as early as one to two years of age. Detailed observations of the mother-child interaction in the homes of these children indicate that the lower class children do not experience the quality of parent-child interaction that occurs in the middle class homes. Specifically, the lower class mothers spend less time in face to face mutual vocalization and smiling with their infants; they do not reward the child's maturational progress, and they do not enter into long periods of play with the child. Our theory of mental development suggests that specific absence of these experiences will retard mental growth and will lead to lower intelligence test scores. The most likely determinants of the black child's lower IQ score are his experiences during the first five years of life. These experiences lead the young black child to do poorly on IQ tests in part because he does not appreciate the nature of a problem.

Kagan's views were echoed by Professor J. McV. Hunt, professor of psychology at the University of Illinois, who felt that Jensen had prefaced his article with a dangerous half-truth: "Compensatory education has been tried and it apparently has failed." Insisting that Jensen had unfairly made Project Head Start synonymous with all compensatory education, Hunt said,

"I find it hard to forgive Professor Jensen for that half-truth placed out of context for dramatic effect at the beginning of his paper." He also challenged the notion that the blacks' lower IQ scores were gentically determined.

Jensen received at least partial support from such fellow academicians as James F. Crow, University of Wisconsin; Carl Bereiter, the Ontario Institute for Studies in Education; David Elkind, University of Rochester; and Lee J. Cronbach, Stanford University. But he was the subject of violent protests in numerous letters addressed to *HER*, one of which came from Professor William F. Brazziel of Virginia State College:

...Last week, a scant five days after Arthur Jensen made headlines in Virginia papers regarding inferiority of black people as measured by IQ tests, defense attorneys and their witnesses fought a suit in the Federal District Court to integrate Greensville and Caroline County schools. Their main argument was that "white teachers could not understand the Nigra mind" and that the Nigra children should not be admitted to the white schools only on the basis of standardized tests. Those who failed to make a certain score would be assigned to all-black remedial schools where "teachers who understood them could work with them." *The defense in this case quoted heavily from the theories of white intellectual supremacy as expounded by Arthur Jensen.*

It will help not one bit for Jensen or the *Harvard Educational Review* editorial board to protest they did not intend for Jensen's article to be used in this way.... Jensen and the *HER* editorial board will modestly admit that they have superior intellects and I am sure they realized the probable consequences of their actions. Questions now arise as to why they decided to raise this issue, in this way, and at this time....

Aside from such letters to *HER*, there were thousands of letters-to-the-editor addressed to scores of newspapers in every state, many of which condemned not only *HER* but also Harvard itself for allowing Jensen's article to be published. There were also numerous editorials, pro and con, and countless discussion shows on television—with the name of Harvard constantly repeated, more often than not leaving the impression that Jensen's views had been tacitly approved by the nation's most prestigious university.

Needless to say, Harvard did not approve or disapprove Jensen's article. Like most universities, it has scrupulously avoided official approval or disapproval of any theories or ideas proposed by its faculty or published in any of the various journals that emanate from the university. Consequently, in view of its traditional espousal of intellectual freedom, one would not expect prior censorship of Jensen or any other academician. Still, as one senior professor recently observed, "This so-called Harvard mystique imposes certain responsibilities on all of us. We can't ignore the fact that some people attach a lot of importance (often too much importance) to anything that comes out of this sanctum sanctorum. So I guess we ought to exert some self-discipline. But who in the hell is going to say how and when?"

In 1973, about three years after Jensen's article appeared, Harvard was once again the focus of a furor regarding educational reform. The specific cause of this controversy was a book written by Cristopher Jencks, a Harvard professor associated with the Cambridge Policy Studies Institute, and several colleagues. Bearing a title more suited to a doctoral thesis, *Inequality: A Reassessment of the Effect of Family and Schooling in America*, this instant best seller and its author were introduced to the public at a sumptious reception at the Waldorf Astoria, where attending book critics were constantly reminded of Jencks' connection to Harvard. Full-page ads in *The New York Times* and a summary in *Saturday Review* also emphasized his Harvard ties.

Enlarging the data base previously used in the Coleman Report, the book concluded that the schools had failed to equalize both short-term achievement levels among children and long-term levels of educational attainment and adult income. Thus, if equality between rich and poor, between black and white children, were an abiding social goal, Jencks and his co-workers felt that it could not be achieved through the schools or any type of compensatory education.

In the stormy debate that followed this pronouncement, the editor of the *Harvard Educational Review* immediately requested critiques from several prominent social scientists, including a panel of ten black scholars from various eastern universities. This latter group met in New York, discussed the book in considerable detail and thereafter delegated Harvard professor Ronald Edmonds to draft their joint response. "In recent years," Edmonds wrote, "public perspective on American social science has been dominated by a species of inquiry most notably characterized by the published works of Coleman, Moynihan, and Jensen. These otherwise dissimilar individuals share the dubious honor of offering observations that sustain or encourage those who would reverse the national momentum of social reform. The Coleman "Report" disparaged a decade of educational intervention on behalf of black children. Moynihan recommended 'benign neglect' of national issues of race. Jensen concluded that black children are educationally disadvantaged by reason of genetic inferiority. Christopher Jencks' recent published *Inequality* is the latest on this list of nay-saying social science observations."

Then, after a point-by-point refutation of Jencks' methodology and *a priori* assumptions, Edmonds declared, "Neither Christopher Jencks nor his ideological forebears will dissuade black advocates from their commitment to educational equity. We never defined educational success as a synonym for social or economic success and therefore have no illusion about the limited role of public instruction in the redress of black grievance. Even so, it is well to point out to polemicists like Jencks that we reserve for outselves the right to decide the criteria for determining when, and whether, public instruction is fulfilling its obligation to poor and black children."

There were numerous other critiques of the book, pro and con, by black and white educators and government officials—but few were as pungent as the *HER* article by Dr. Kenneth B. Clark, who pointedly alluded to the fact that Jencks' Harvard professorship would give his book added (and unmerited) status in the eyes of federal and state policymakers in the field of education. After reviewing several prior criticisms of compensatory programs for disadvantaged children, Clark wrote:

Probably the most sophisticated recent contribution to this counsel of despair is the Christopher Jencks and associates report on *Inequality: A Reassessment of the Effect of Family and Schooling in America.* My analysis of the book will not address the problems of methodology, accuracy of the findings, or the relationship between alleged findings on the one hand, and interpretations and conclusions on the other. Neither is this analysis primarily concerned with the irritating problem of Jencks' style of presentation. However, it is the judgment of this writer that there is a serious question of propriety when a well-publicized document, which deals with the important issue of racial equality in public education, is presented in an essentially glib, journalistic, smart-alecky manner. The consequences of social scientists dealing with matters of equity and justice through the exploitation of Madison Avenue advertising techniques is a problem which must be faced by serious social scientists and their professional organizations. Jencks' findings and interpretations had been skillfully advertised to the general public through the mass media before other social scientists had had the opportunity to review them critically. By the time this study could be carefully reviewed, the general public, including policy makers, was quoting Jencks' questionable findings as if they were sacred writ. This process highlights a new, fashionable, and most disturbing approach: a group of social scientists, having mastered the art of public relations, are able to confuse scientific validation with effective mass publicity. Given that the mass media have an insatiable need for sensational findings and that journalists are not usually trained to make critical appraisals of the claims of scientists, it is not difficult for the skillful social scientist–public relations expert to phrase his "findings" in such a way as to become an overnight celebrity. *When this is supported by the name of a prestigious university* [author's italics] and by the backup of the infallible computer, the public's uncritical acceptance of the Olympian utterances of the celebrity social scientist is practically guaranteed. This approach makes for seemingly interesting discussions on TV talk shows, but is clearly questionable science.

One should note that Jencks had once before incurred the wrath of black scholars when he and David Riesman co-authored an article on "The American Negro College," published in the 1967 winter issue of the *Harvard Educational Review*. Stating that "public Negro colleges are for the most part likely to remain fourth-rate institutions at the tail end of the academic procession," the two Harvard professors further said, "Despite the affluence of the public Negro colleges relative to most private ones, both in terms of salaries and working conditions, these institutions will have an extremely difficult time competing for competent faculty—and an even more difficult time persuading whatever faculty they get to deal with their students in an imaginative way. These colleges have very little to tempt a talented professor, whatever his color...."

Although some black educators readily conceded that such colleges were less than satisfactory, they nevertheless felt it was counterproductive for *HER* to focus a spotlight on this particular issue. As one of them remarked in a private conversation, "This article simply gives the bigots a chance to bolster their contention that blacks are inherently inferior. And they'll be referring to 'these here Harvard professors'—even though the authors say nothing about racial inferiority."

Aside from the positive and/or negative influence of *HER*, the ed school's faculty and alumni have strongly influenced educational policies and administrative practices throughout the United States and several foreign countries. The school's roster boasts two former U.S. commissioners of education, two directors of the National Institute of Education, several state commissioners of education, over 170 superintendents of schools (including the districts of Dallas, Chicago, San Francisco, Washington, D.C., Rochester, Birmingham, Tacoma, Atlanta,

Ottawa, Albany, *et al.*), seventy-eight associate or assistant superintendents, 203 principals or headmasters, twenty-one college or university presidents (other branches of Harvard have produced more than 150 presidents), sixty deans or associate deans, at least forty-five chairmen of faculty departments, and several presidents of educational foundations. It has also produced the crossword puzzle editor of *The New York Times.*

Moreover, through its Center for Studies in Education and Development (CSED), the school has trained professors and administrators for school systems in Iraq, Saudi Arabia, Nigeria, Mexico, Iran, Japan, Brazil, Ghana, Colombia, Puerto Rico, Spain, Malasia, Senegal, Kuwait and many other Third World nations. Indeed, as one visitor recently remarked on passing through the school's Gutman Library, "This looks like the United Nations."

The ed school has a higher percentage of blacks, Chicanos, American Indians, and Orientals than any other branch of the university. It also has a higher percentage of women students, some of whom participated in an all-female team that conducted an NIMH-funded study of "forty-three women and 5,000 variables," which was the highlight at a conference on family stress in low-income groups at the Aspen Institute for Humanistic Studies. The research team was directed by Dr. Deborah Belle.

Speaking of research, one should not fail to mention the work of Dr. Burton White, whose very readable best-selling book *The First Three Years* has been read by hundreds of thousands of parents in both the hard- and soft-cover editions. Among his many other accomplishments, White has made a major contribution to the Brookline Early Education Project (BEEP), a model program for teaching mothers how to stimulate the cognitive and emotional growth of their infants. BEEP and White were the subject of a cover article in *The New York Times Sunday Magazine.*

It has been said around Cambridge that one should never

invite Dr. White to the same party with Professor Jerome Bruner
or Professor Jerome S. Kagan, his archrivals in the field of infant
development: "There is no room in town that can accommodate
more than one of these prima donnas," says one old-timer, "not
unless you can deflate their heads by at least 50%."

Asked to comment on Bruner and Kagan at an informal lunch,
White offhandedly referred to Bruner's well-known research
apparatus as "Jerry's funny little toys."

As the then director of the prestigious Center for Cognitive
Studies and no doubt aware that he ranked much higher in
Harvard's pecking order than White, the soft-spoken Bruner*
airily dismissed any serious discussion of White's intellectual
endeavors. "After all," one of his colleagues later remarked,
"you can't expect Jerry to be concerned about a mere ed school
professor."

*Bruner has since left Harvard to join the faculty of Oxford University.

To lead the nation into battle, the President chose 49-year-old James Rodney Schlesinger, a Harvard-educated economist, former college professor, avid bird-watcher and baseball buff.

A sort of cabinet-level utility infielder, Schlesinger seems equally comfortable serving Democrats or Republicans. Before President Carter named him to organize and head the new Department of Energy (DOE), Schlesinger served previous Republican administrations as assistant budget director, chairman of the Atomic Energy Commission, director of the Central Intelligence Agency and Secretary of Defense until President Ford—with whom he shared a deep, mutual dislike—fired him from the Pentagon job in November 1975.

—Michael Satchell,
*Parade* magazine

# CHAPTER X The Arab Connection at Harvard: Money Equals Power

LESS THAN A TWO-MINUTE WALK from Harvard Square, in the dimly lit basement of the ancient Brattle Theatre, there is a nightly gathering of Arab students from various branches of the university. Their haven is called the Algeria Coffee House, which serves thick black coffee and unleavened Syrian bread that is most appropriate for thoughtful munching and intensely serious conversation about the never-ending conflicts of the Middle East.

Huddled around each small table one is apt to find a curious mix of Arab scholars—the expensively dressed son of an unimaginably rich shah from Saudi Arabia, the lovely daughter of an impecunious Iraqi schoolteacher, the bright-eyed son of a shepherd from South Yemen, and the nervously intense son of a Lebanese banker—yet they all seem to be ineluctably bound together by common fears, common hatreds and a deeply felt reverence for "the Arab cause."

Some day, perhaps in ten or fifteen years, these young Arabs will come into positions of great power and immense wealth in their respective countries, and some of their fellow students from

Denver or Atlanta will say, "My God, I used to sit next to that
guy in Professor Leontief's course on economic theory, but I
never dreamed he had that kind of potential." No doubt such
statements have been made about the somewhat smaller number
of Arab students who (during the early '60s.) met regularly
every Sunday afternoon at a Chinese restaurant near the Yard.
There was no Algiers Coffee House in those days, nor any other
specifically Arabic restaurant within the confines of the Harvard
community, so they had to settle for the ubiquitous cuisine of
China, even though their always-intense discussions were keenly
focused on the volatile Arab-Israeli conflict.

Among these Sunday-afternoon regulars were four graduate
students who were destined to exercise control over a vast
financial empire: Abdlatif al-Hamad, the brilliant son of a
wealthy Kuwait merchant, who was attending Professor Kissinger's famous seminar; Ibrahim F.I. Shihata, a quiet-spoken,
scholarly Egyptian who was acquiring a doctorate in jurispru-
dence at Harvard Law School; H.R. Shohaty, a shepherd's son
from South Yemen, who was studying for a doctorate in
economics; and Jalal Amin, an easy-going but penetratingly
intelligent Iraqi who was also in Kissinger's doctoral program in
government.

None of these men had known one another until they got to
Cambridge, but they were soon drawn into a tightly knit
"intelligentsia within an intelligentsia," their interests ranging
from ancient Persian poetry to the socioeconomic aspects of the
oil boom. According to law school professor Richard Baxter,
who was a sort of academic godfather to several Arab students
and was occasionally invited to one of their Sunday-afternoon
suppers, "Their conversations were passionate and eclectic,
sharply analytic and yet permissively broad, a marvelous brew of
erudition and humor. I never for one moment doubted that each
one of them would someday play a major role in the Middle
East."

Only one of the four, Abdlatif al-Hamad, failed to get a doctoral degree, but he seems to have been more Harvardized than any of his cohorts. Having received his elementary and preparatory education at the prestigious Victoria School in Alexandria (often called the Arab Eton because of its supra-British orientation), al-Hamad received his undergraduate training at Claremont College in California. "But my ultimate goal was always Harvard," he readily admits to friends and strangers alike. "In my way of thinking, all roads led to Cambridge." Graduating *magna cum laude* at Claremont, he had no difficulty getting admitted to the graduate school of government at Harvard, where he studied with such determination and single-minded intensity that he never once moved his newly purchased sports car from his assigned parking space behind Perkins Hall. "I had no time, nor disposition, for extracurricular frivolity—except for our Sunday-afternoon supper seminars."

Consequently, to no one's surprise, he received straight A's in all his courses for the first year and finally permitted himself the luxury of a projected summer vacation in New York. But ten days after his arrival in Manhattan he ran into some old friends from Kuwait, who had come to the United States to present a petition for their country's admission to the United Nations. "You've got to help us draft the papers, Abdlatif," one of them insisted. "You write English much better than any of us." Reluctantly foergoing his vacation plans, al-Hamad agreed to help them; then later, having requested a leave of absence from the fall semester at Harvard, he spearheaded the eventually successful presentation of Kuwait's petition for admission.

Obviously impressed with his diplomatic and administrative skills, the prime minister of Kuwait asked al-Hamad to help draft plans for what was to become the Kuwait Fund for Arab Economic Development. So once again—much against the advice of Shihata, Shohaty and Amin—he asked for another leave of absence from his graduate studies. Then, as if fate had decreed against his academic future, the director of the newly created fund suffered a heart attack and died soon thereafter. Unable to resist internal political pressures, al-Hamad at the ripe old age of twenty-four "provisionally agreed" to serve as director for a year or two, but he stayed on and on as the fund escalated from several hundred million dollars to more than $3 billion. Meanwhile, his good friends received their Ph.D. degrees and returned to their respective countries: Shihata to a low-paying professorship at the University of Cairo; Amin to a government post in Iraq, Shohaty to a modest-salaried job as a development economist in South Yemen.

But when the Kuwait Fund (which functions like an amalgam of the Ford Foundation and the World Bank) became the largest institution of its kind in the entire world, with huge development loans all over the Middle East, its still-young (thirty-eight years old) director persuaded his former Harvard "schoolmates" to join his staff. Thus, Shihata is now general legal counsel, Shohaty directs the economic planning division and Amin is head of the political affairs sections—and they are collectively known as "the brain trust" of Kuwait and quite possibly of the entire Arab region.

Nevertheless, although he is one of the most powerful financiers in the world (and the boss of three old friends who got the doctoral degree he once sought), al-Hamad often says, "My one big regret is leaving Harvard without getting my Ph.D. As a matter of fact, I think that anyone who gets admitted to one of the graduate schools should automatically get some kind of degree, because getting admitted is really three-fourths of the battle."

Even more influential than al-Hamad is a fellow Arab from Saudi Arabia, whose name became a difficult-to-pronounce household word when the 1974 oil embargo caused an enormous upheaval in the world economy. He is Ahmed Zaki Yamani, a Harvard Law School graduate (1966) who serves as minister of oil of the country which dominates the petroleum industry.

Along with several other Arab students, Yamani studied international law under Professor Manley Hudson, former chief justice of the International Court at The Hague. Indeed, it was Professor Hudson and two of his Harvard protégés who set up the legal framework for ARAMCO, the Arabian-American Oil Company, which has a major control of world oil production. Recently, Yamani negotiated a $2 billion purchase of foreign-held shares in ARAMCO, thus giving Saudi Arabia complete ownership of it oil facilities.

It should be noted that *The New York Times* financial section recently named "the four most important non-Arab figures in the oil industry," two of whom are former professors at the Harvard Business School: Thorton F. Bradshaw, president of Atlantic Richfield, and John G. McLean, chairman of the giant Continental Oil. But the *Times* goes on to say that "real power in the oil world rests with the Arabs, particularly with their most creative thinker—Sheik Ahmed Zaki Yamani."

While studying at the Harvard Law School, Yamani met and became a close friend of Amir Ambari, an astute and very scholarly Arab from Iraq. Less than a decade later, when OPEC (Oil Producers Economic Council) was formed as the all-powerful principal combine of the oil-producing nations, Yamani easily persuaded his fellow ministers to retain his classmate as general counsel, thus reaffirming the incestuous advantages of attending the right law school.

With his OPEC connection, Ambari has become the most influential lawyer in Iraq, but one never knows what the future holds for anyone in the volatile Arab countries. Take, for example, the case of Naizir Jawdat, who lived a life of opulent luxury while earning his degree in architecture at the Harvard School of Design, his father then serving as Iraq's ambassador in Washington, D.C. Later on, when his father became prime minister, young Jawdat became Iraq's leading architect and city planner. But when the *ancien régime* was dethroned by a leftist revolt in the middle '60s, Jawdat fled to Rome and later established a thriving Middle East investment business in London, occasionally dealing with fabulously rich "cousins" from Abu Dahbi or one of the other oil-rich emirates, some of whom he had met in Cambridge.

Although Harvard men profoundly influence the internal and external affairs of Kuwait and Saudi Arabia, the Harvard presence seems more apparent in Iran. In the suburban rim of bustling Teheran one will find the dazzling modern structures of Iran's Graduate School of Business and Management, where thousands of Iranians and hundreds of Arabs from all sectors of the Middle East are learning the most up-to-date practices of business and finance. This graduate center was initially organized and staffed by professors and graduates of the Harvard Business School, and the symbiotic relationship between the two institutions has been carefully nurtured by a constant interchange of personnel and information, with HBS professor James McKinney serving as the principal intercessor.

The Cambridge influence will be even more evident when the new University of Iran is completed. With a projected cost of more than $1 billion, the huge university complex is being planned and designed by a team of Harvard architects and urban planners. The dean of the Harvard School of Design, John Kilbridge, and his colleague Professor Hal Goyette, are the principal Cambridge participants. Three Iranian architects (Nader Ardalan, George Kondracki and Mohammed Jadjd), all graduates of Harvard, constitute the Teheran branch of the team. While discussing the project with several reporters, Dean Kilbridge was asked if he had obtained the contract through his former student-protégés from Iran or through some more immediate contact in the Harvard Business School.

"Well, either of those assumptions is certainly logical," he answered. "But the actual truth is that we were recommended for the job by a professor at the Harvard Medical School, who happens to be the personal physician for the shah of Iran. So I guess that's further—though rather oblique—proof of what they say about us Harvard people always scratching each other's back."

Given that premise, one might assume that ex-Cantabrigians should be well received at the Central Bank of Iran, where the legal department is directed by a graduate of the Harvard Law School, Dr. Morteza Nassiri, who has also served as dean of the law school of the University of Iran. They might also wish to do business with Abram Manocherian, a graduate of the Harvard Business School and one of the leading financiers and industrialists of Iran. His son and nephew hope to study along the banks of the Charles River in the near future.

Having deliberately established a "universal constituency" by its systematic attraction of students from almost every country in the world, Harvard has been especially alluring for Arab students who wanted to avoid the so-called Oxford syndrome. Until three or four decades ago, the sons of wealthy Middle East families usually received their preparatory training at the Victoria School in Alexandria, and thereafter finished their education at Oxford or Cambridge University.

But, as one prominent Egyptian recently said, "Some of us wanted to break that colonial tie."

Consequently, in the summer of 1946 six Egyptian students, who laughingly called themselves "the Arab pilgrims," boarded an old merchant ship in Alexandria and set sail for the far-off port of Boston. They had each received fellowships to Harvard (with modest stipends for room and board), and a few years later they graduated from various divisions of the university and subsequently became prominent leaders in the political, legal, educational and financial circles of Egypt.

Dr. Aziz Zidky, who earned his graduate degree in town planning at the Harvard School of Design (architecture), served several administrations as an urban specialist and later became prime minister.

Dr. Mohammed Merzban, who received his degree in political science, had a dual career as a professor at Cairo University and as a governmental administrator. He was eventually appointed deputy prime minister, by his "fellow pilgrim" and Harvard classmate, Dr. Zidky.

Dr. S. Ashraf Gohrbal, graduate of both Harvard College and the law school, served in various governmental and diplomatic posts and later became a close advisor of Anwar Sadat. It was Gohrbal who brilliantly negotiated a rapprochement between Egypt and the United States, thus healing a protracted diplomatic rift between the two nations. To no one's surprise, Sadat appointed Gohrbal as ambassador to Washington, where he has served with distinction for six years, frequently functioning as a becalmer of troubled waters whenever a new Middle East crisis approaches floodtide. An avid Harvardian who remembers his years in Cambridge with nostalgic affection, he visits New England frequently and seldom misses the Harvard–Yale game.

Dr. Zaki Hashem, also a graduate of the Harvard Law School, became dean of the law school at Cairo University, then relinquished his academic post to become a senior partner in Egypt's most prestigious law firm.

Dr. Yehya El Molla, who received his Ph.D. in economics at Harvard, where his favorite teacher was Professor Wassily Leontief, became Egypt's most influential economist and has been a personal adviser to Nasser and Sadat.

Ghassan Tweini, the only one of the six "Arab pilgrims" who did not obtain a Ph.D., completed his required residence courses but had to leave Harvard before completing his doctoral dissertation to take over the family business when his father died. He has since become a leading industrialist and financier.

Most of these six prominent Arabs remember their sojourn at Harvard with mixed feelings. There were periods of easy camaraderie with non-Arabs, some of which led to lifelong friendships; but there were also periods of deep hostility and alienation. The state of Israel came into being in the late '40s, and its emergence provoked prolonged and furious debates between Arab and Jewish students. Unfortunately, that hostile situation still exists, perhaps exacerbated by the Arabs' new sense of economic power. *Time* magazine (Nov. 19, 1975) described the current ambiance as follows:

To the Arabs at universities across the country, America is a land where they are at best misunderstood and at worst harassed and insulted. More serious than any personal affront is the condescension to all things Arab that both students and scholars think infects American scholarship as well.

The Middle East programs, from which American students get their knowledge of Arab society, go back to the 18th century, when Hebrew and Arabic were valued for their relevance to biblical and archaeological studies. They have thrived in recent years with funds from the post-Sputnik National Defense Education Act, the Ford Foundation and oil companies. Today leading centers—generally umbrella departments coordinating language, history, cultural and political studies—are at Princeton, UCLA, Columbia, Chicago, Berkeley, Harvard and Michigan.

Arabs charge that these centers are beset by a condition known as "Arablessness," and that this in turn gives American students a distorted, outsiders' view of Arab culture. A major manifestation is a lack of scholars from the Arab world, particularly in contemporary studies. Harvard, for instance, has three Arabs on its tenured faculty, but two are medievalists and the third is a linguist. There are no tenured Arabs at all in the University of Chicago's Middle Eastern program, and only one in a staff of 15 at Berkeley.

The few Arab scholars who are here often find their role awkward or ambiguous, and a comparison with the situation of blacks in major U.S. universities ten years ago is not outlandish. Northwestern Political Scientist Ibrahim Abu-Lughod, a Palestinian, dismisses many Arab professors here as "Uncle Ahmeds" who are treated as mere "native informants" rather than experts.

Many universities despair of finding a qualified Arab who would be willing to settle into what they admit is a hostile environment. Says the director of Harvard's center, Turkish Anthropologist Nur Yalman: "Arabs who are educated enough to compete in the environment of the Western university are already the cream of the cream." He adds that such men have a "serious consciousness of a deep cultural gap between the Christian and the Moslem worlds."

The center's assistant director, A.J. Meyer, also concedes Harvard's relatively Arabless state and notes that "all our students have the impression that some kind of plot is working against their point of view." The loudest complaints are about the lack of courses in modern, colloquial Arabic, contemporary social and economic problems, and the Arab viewpoint on the Middle Eastern crisis.

The fact that among students and faculty there are few Arabs—and many Jews—at Harvard aggravates Arab feelings of isolation. Senior Omar Rifai, a Jordanian, feels more like an object of curiosity than discrimination, but he claims that he still has to listen to some of his professors say "that the Arabs are cowardly, that we live in tents."

Wilson, with his brilliant scholarly reputation and Harvard credentials, has both the visibility and credibility to legitimate the biological approach to sociology.

—Alan Mazur,
*American Journal of Sociology,*
June 1976

# CHAPTER XI  The Controversial Science

As ONE MIGHT EXPECT from a university that thrives on intellectual crossfires, Harvard has produced more than its share of controversial scholars, and some of their theories have had a profound influence on governmental policies that have affected millions of lives. Several years ago, for example, as mentioned in a previous chapter, Professor B. F. Skinner created a furor throughout this country and Europe with his highly disturbing concept that human beings are pliable creatures whose behavior can be almost entirely shaped by their environment—all of which sparked heated objections from certain intellectuals who unreasonably and too readily accused Skinner of proposing "a fascistic manipulation" of innocent people.

More recently, Professor Edward Wilson has aroused the wrath of traditional liberals and leftists with his diametrically opposite theory that most human traits and behavior are genetically determined, that environment is a negligible factor. Thus, according to Wilson's "sociobiology": children are born deceitful; conflicts between parents and children are biologically inevitable; morality and justice, far from being indicia of human progress, are merely survival patterns from man's animal past. In fact, all human acts—even saving a stranger from drowning or giving food to the poor—are deemed to be essentially selfish behavior "securely rooted in the genes." Some of Wilson's fellow sociobiologists suggest that there may be human genes that dictate homosexuality, social conformity and even spite.

Carried to its logical extreme, sociobiology boldly asserts that the sole purpose of all forms of life is to serve DNA, the coded master molecule ("the stuff of the genes") that determines the nature of all organisms. Describing the role and propelling force of genes, British ethologist Richard Dawkins says, "They swarm in huge colonies, safe inside gigantic lumbering robots, sealed off from the outside world, manipulating it by remote control. They are in you and me; they created us body and mind; and their preservation is the ultimate rationale for our existence ... we are their survival machines."

Convinced that genetic forces govern all living matter, the sociobiologists believe it's impossible to study any aspect of human culture without a basic reference to biology. Robert Trivers, a Harvard biologist and a leading proponent of this new theory, confidently predicts, "Sooner or later, political science, law, economics, psychology, psychiatry and anthropology will be branches of sociobiology." Somewhat bemused by Trivers' sweeping optimism, Harvard physicist Gerald Holton says, "It's a breathtaking ambition. It's as if Sigmund Freud had set out to subsume all of Darwin, Joyce, Einstein, Whitehead and Lenin."

Needless to say, the grandiose claims of the sociobiologists have provoked a wide variety of reactions—from angry denunciation to smiling disdain. But the denunciations became more numerous and more passionate in 1975, when Wilson's 700-page *Sociobiology: The New Synthesis* was published. Within a few weeks, its so-called "inflamatory" thesis spread far beyond Cambridge, dividing faculty departments at various universities from coast to coast, and also causing disruptive arguments at usually staid academic conventions. Sneeringly dubbing it "so-so biology," scores of liberal intellectuals have condemned Wilson's theory as "reactionary political doctrine disguised as science." Blacks, Jews, Chicanos and other minority groups are among the most vociferous opponents of sociobiology, which they consider "a blatant form of intellectual racism." In their minds, the sociobiologists' espousal of "genetic determination" inevitably leads to the supposition that certain races are genetically superior while others are *ipso facto* genetically inferior. Realizing that Wilson's and Triver's Harvard credentials will give added weight to their theories ("the ultimate academic stamp of approval"), these critics fear that sociobiology will be used to justify further attacks on open admissions, school integration, affirmative action, and drastic reductions in health-care, education and welfare spending.

Other scholars, particularly Marxists, have criticized sociobiology for different reasons. Jerome Schneewind, a philosopher at Hunter College, disdainfully dismisses it as "a mushy metaphor ... a souped-up version of Hobbes." Marshall Sahlins, an anthropologist at the University of Chicago, characterizes it as "genetic capitalism," a facile justification for the socioeconomic structures of nonsocialist countries. Professor Richard Lewontin, an evolutionary biologist at Harvard, is much more succinct in his criticism of sociobiology: "It's pure bullshit," he says. "But it is not a racist doctrine. Nevertheless, any kind of genetic determinism can and does feed other kinds, including the belief that some races are superior to others."

The furor caused by sociobiology is reminiscent of a similar controversy in 1969 (discussed in Chapter IX) when the *Harvard Educational Review* published Arthur Jensen's revival of the doctrine that blacks are genetically inferior, basing his conclusions on a comparative study of IQ-test scores. Extremely critical of the federal government's efforts to improve black education through remedial programs and busing, Jensen proposed segregated rote learning for black children, which his opponents called "educational apartheid." Having also felt the lash of black leaders for his highly publicized report in "matriarchal ghetto families," Daniel Patrick Moynihan eagerly embraced the basic tenets of Jensen's article. In an interview published in *Life* magazine, the former Harvard Professor happily announced that "the winds of Jensen were gusting through the capital at gale force," and observation that no doubt endeared him to Richard Nixon, whom he was then serving as chief adviser on domestic policy. (Soon thereafter Moynihan wrote a your-eyes-only secret memorandum to the president in which he proposed a policy of "benign neglect" with respect to the ever-worsening problems of black people, a proposal that would later cause a benign ostracism of Moynihan by his former colleagues at Harvard.)

Although most of the Cambridge community rejected Jensen's views, there were a few professors who avidly supported them. In an article published in *Atlantic Monthly* in 1971, psychologist Richard Herrnstein extended the assertion of genetic inferiority to all working-class people. And a year later, Herrnstein joined Jensen and forty-seven colleagues in a resolution published in *American Psychologist* in which they compared themselves to Galileo, Darwin and Einstein, and airily condemned the "orthodox environmentalism" of social scientists who disagreed with them. Declaring that hereditary influences in human abilities and behavior "are very strong," they deplored "the evasion of hereditary reasoning in current textbooks and the failure to give responsible weight to heredity in disciplines such as sociobiology, social psychology, social anthropology, psychological measurement, and many others." As a countermeasure, they urgently proposed immediate and extensive "research into the biological hereditary bases of human behavior."

Several months later, the Committee Against Racism (initially organized by several Harvard professors) circulated a resolution condemning Jensen's IQ theories as racist and unscientific. CAR further declared that the Jensen-Herrnstein doctrines were legitimating racial oppression and inequality, whether or not they blamed the victim's class or race. With more than 1,000 signatures of scholars throughout the country, the committee published its resolution in *The New York Times* on October 28, 1973. One of the signers was Professor Leon Kamin, a Princeton psychologist who was meanwhile analyzing all the data and studies that Jensen and other hereditarians had used in their ethnic evaluations of IQ scores. Proponents of hereditary determination had relied heavily on studies of identical twins reared apart, but Kamin and his colleagues were able to prove that the studies were absolutely worthless—that without appropriate controls the researchers' final correlations could just as easily reflect environmental or hereditary influences. The only study which seemed to have controls for enviornmental factors had been conducted by Sir Cyril Burt, an English psychologist; but Kamin soon realized that Burt's data "had to be cooked." In three articles published during an eleven-year span, with his "sample" of identical-twins-reared-apart expanding by 150%, Burt reported a correlation in IQ scores that remained amazingly constant to three decimal places (.771). Had any other research reported such a "strange imperturbability" in results, he would have been accused of cheating—yet in 1976 the American Psychological Association awarded Burt its highest prize. Shortly thereafter, much to the chagrin of APA officials, the London *Times* finally exposed Burt as an outright fraud (October 24, 1976). In a front-page article, an investigative reporter revealed that Burt's two co-authors, who had been credited with administering the IQ tests, had never existed.

Momentarily set back by the Burt fiasco, the hereditarians have nevertheless continued their propagation of the faith. In a recent issue of *Annual Review of Genetics,* one of the main articles on the "genetics of cognitive behavior" has favorable comments on some of the ever-increasing literature on genetic inequality. The article also sharply criticizes Professor Richard Lewontin for his unrelenting condemnation of the Jensen–Herrnstein studies.

But Lewontin and many of his Harvard colleagues are even more concerned about the sociobiologists whose theories have been an enormous boost for hereditary doctrine. Although he himself has dismissed sociobiology as "pure bullshit," Lewontin sadly realizes that it has been gaining wide acceptance, chiefly because of its "Harvard connection." *Sociobiology: The New Synthesis* was published and heavily promoted by the Harvard University Press; and its forty-eight-year-old author, Edward Wilson, is curator of entomology at Harvard's Museum of Comparative Zoology—"a double portion of the Harvard mystique," in the words of one critic, who also noted that Wilson and his fellow sociobiologists were the subjects of a nine-page cover story in *Time* magazine (August 1977).

Showing the article to one of his associates at the U.S. Department of Health, Education and Welfare, a high-ranking official pessimistically observed, "This is the kind of stuff that budget-cutters like to quote when they want to get rid of remedial programs for minority children. That fancy Harvard label gives them all the ammunition they want—and they'll quote some of these professors, even if they don't really understand their goddam theories and doctrines."

Sociobiologists refer to their doctrine as "the completion of the Darwinian revolution"—the joint application of modern genetics and classic evolutionary theory to the behavior of animals and human beings. Now rarely challenged in the scientific community, Darwin's theory states that all organisms evolve by natural selection, that only those better adapted to their environments will survive and reproduce, while the rest perish. Presumably improved by the fierce competitive struggle for survival, such organisms are considered "the winners in the evolutionary game"—and the sociobiologists believe that the patterns of winning behavior are transmitted by the genes to succeeding generations.

Although Darwin's "natural selection" theory referred to *individual* organisms, more recent scholars (Konrad Lorenz, the

Nobel laureate ethologist, and biologist V.C. Wynne-Edwards) have nominated the *species* or *group* as the unit of natural selection. Proposing a narrower, more specific focus, the Harvard-based sociobiologists believe that the genes themselves play the dominant roles in the evolutionary drama. And their theory of genetic transmittal seems to be supported by recent research in an entirely different field of science. Professor George Pieczenik, a Rutgers University biochemist, claims to have discovered certain patterns in DNA coding that suggest a process of natural selection at the molecular level. "The DNA sequences exist to protect themselves and their own information," says Pieczenik.

In a restricted sense, his findings seem to echo Darwin's theory that every organism fights for its own survival and the chance to reproduce, with no concern for other organisms. But Darwin could not account for the occasional altruistic behavior of some organisms, which help other members of their species at the risk of their own survival. Spotting an enemy hawk, certain birds will loudly squawk to warn the flock, thus risking the special and murderous attention of the hawk. Researchers have observed "social insects" drudgingly serving an entire colony, sometimes sacrificing their lives to protect their fellow insects from invading enemies. Indeed, similar protective behavior has been rooted in various species of animals and (perhaps less frequently) in human beings.

One might reasonably assume that such behavioral patterns are *learned* from older members of any given group, but socio-biologists firmly believe that they are transmitted by genes—that altruism is actually "genetic selfishness." Thus, according to Wilson and his cohorts at Harvard, when the bird squawks a warning that an enemy hawk is approaching, it is merely protecting its close relatives, thereby increasing the survivability of their mutual genes. No one has offered any specific proof that birds are even remotely conscious of their own genes, nor has anyone mentioned the possibility that the bird squawks because it's scared and is merely concerned about its own safety. But the sociobiologists are not easily deterred by an absence of verifiable data and are apparently content to reason by analogy, especially when they can draw an analogy between insects and human beings.

One of their favorite examples is the 1964 study of the social life of insects by biologist William Hamilton, who eventually concluded that altruism could enable an individual to spread his genes "the way insects do." Referring to ants, bees and wasps, Hamilton says that the female offspring of the queen share an average of 75% of their genes. Consequently, since the daughters are more genetically related to each other than they would be to their own progeny, it is in their genetic self-interest to forego breeding and to help the queen produce more females. Thus, sterile female insects work and sacrifice their own lives to promote the dissemination of the genes they share with sister ants.

Having carefully studied Hamilton's data, Robert Trivers thereafter hypothesized that worker ants would apply three times as much energy rearing sisters as rearing brothers, since the female workers were more closely related to their sisters by a ratio of 3 to 1. With the help of Hope Hare, a Harvard colleague, Trivers conducted a massive analysis of thousands of ants of twenty different species and subsequently announced that they had "confirmed" a female dominance of 3 to 1, which he claimed was "the strongest evidence so far that organisms act as if they understand their own underlying genetics."

Emboldened by such evidence of genetic altruism (or self-interest), Trivers was unable to curb his penchant for simplistic analogies between insect behavior and human behavior: "In other organisms," he wrote in 1971, "the evidence that altruism is genetic is rather overwhelming. It is therefore irrational to argue that the first species in which altruism has no genetic contribution is human beings."

One might assume from that sweeping statement that Trivers

and/or his fellow sociobiologists have actually studied thousands of other nonhuman species, with unanimous evidence of genetic altruism—but there have been very few extensive studies, and they have been confined to insects, fish and other simple organisms. (For instance, most of Wilson's research at Harvard has been restricted to insects, particularly ants.)

Yet, in spite of their minimal and extremely limited evidence, the sociobiologists have shown no hesitancy in their facile comparisons of insect and human behavior. Consequently, they seem to have explanations for almost every aspect of human conduct, and their explanations tend to be put-downs. Maternal love is viewed as a method for ensuring genetic survival. Human friendships are merely "reciprocal altruism" or mutual survival techniques that are rooted in our genes. "We are likely to see some of our most exalted feelings explained in terms of traits which are genetically evolved," says Wilson. "We may find that there is an overestimation of the nature of our deepest yearnings."

Such human yearnings, say the sociobiologists, are so clouded with rationalizations and self-deceit that they should be re-examined with a cool scientific eye. Indeed, Wilson has proposed that "ethics be removed temporarily from the hands of philosophers and biologized." Although his definition of a "biologized ethic" is rather fuzzy, he apparently suggests that moral standards for males might be different from those for females— that adults and children may also have different ethics. He believes, for example, that the ethic of children includes a genetically based resistance to parental control, and that there may be a genetic mandate for teenagers to hang out together and to set their own rules of conduct.

Since joining a gang and bugging Mom and Dad are just as likely prime examples of behavior learned after birth—learned from older siblings or one's culture—Wilson's reasoning seems rather narrow and myopic, perhaps the inevitable result of prolonged confinement in a research laboratory.

"It's the most incredible crap I've ever heard," said a UCLA professor when informed of Wilson's and Trivers' novel speculations. "Those Harvard ant experts sound crazy as hell. They must have been mesmerized by all those thousands of ants, so that they've finally taken on the intellectual characteristics of their fucking ants! That's about the only explanation I can think of for all this nonsense they're putting out. But just because they're from Harvard, you'll see all kinds of so-called scholars accepting their crap—even some of the professors on this campus. If some researcher at Podunk University tried to peddle the same theories, he'd be laughed out of town and booted off the faculty—but if you've got that Harvard label you can sell anything to the natives."

In a somewhat calmer tone, a Columbia University professor also regretted the fact that sociobiology is blessed with the imprimatur of Harvard. "Let's face it," he said to one of his graduate students, "no matter how specious and even silly they sound, these sociobiologists are going to get a lot of serious attention and perhaps ultimate approval—and only because they're from Harvard. And I really wouldn't care too much if their theories were merely academic—mere philosophic speculations—but I'm afraid they'll be taken seriously by people in Washington, by reactionary congressmen who will say, 'There's no sense trying to improve things for blacks and Puerto Ricans with all these expensive remedial programs. We can't change their genes.' And they'll be able to quote 'this here Harvard professor' to back their prejudices."

As we have had occasion to note several times before in other chapters, Harvard does not officially approve or disapprove the research or theories of any member of its faculty. Its professors are presumably free to think as they please, however unpopular their thinking may be. But like any other university, it can and *does* exercise some degree of thought control through its power to withhold tenure. And in the case of Robert Trivers, the university did indeed exercise this option by rejecting his bid for tenure in the spring of 1977. Although university officials deny that his work in sociobiology was the reason, Trivers and his supporters regard this "invitation to leave Cambridge" as a not too subtle form of academic repression. "But I don't think they will be successful in stopping me or slowing down the work," Trivers later remarked. "It has spread too far, to too many people, and to far. too many studies."

While Trivers will no longer have the benefit of a Harvard platform for his controversial theories, the grand mandarin of sociobiology, Edward Wilson, is still at the university and (with full tenure) can remain there as long as he pleases—subject, of course, to mandatory retirement at the age of sixty-five. Still his life inside or outside the ivy-covered Yard is not likely to be tranquil. The publication of his book caused a furor among students and faculty alike, many of whom called it "dangerously racist" and threatened to picket his laboratory.

One black undergradute smilingly suggested that someone should kidnap a pan of Wilson's ants, but the tight security around the Museum of Comparative Zoology would have thwarted such a caper. Nevertheless, the aborted scheme gave rise to the quip that "Professor Wilson has ants in his pans."

As for his critics' charge of "racism," Wilson does suggest a "certain plausibility" in the notion that social classes reflect genetic differences and that the upper classes may gradually accumulate a pool of superior genes—but he readily admits that there is "little evidence" of such superiority, citing the fact that even the 2,000-year-old castes of India seem not to show any measurable genetic differences. Nevertheless, he still believes there is "a loose correlation of some of the genetically determined traits with success," somewhat vaguely hinting that 10% or 15% of human behavior is based on genetic evolution. When informed of Wilson's statistical speculations, Sahlins mockingly wondered if the Harvard sociobiologist could attribute human behavior to "10% biology, 5% physics, 3% chemistry, .07% geology, 81% symbolic logic and .3% the action of heavenly bodies."

Sahlin and Lewontin may continue to mock Wilson, but his

academic support inside and outside Cambridge is formidable.
Among the more avid converts to sociobiology is Harvard's
Irven DeVore, one of America's leading anthropologists, who
has decided to "redo" all of his major primate studies pursuant to
the tenets of the "new science."

Meanwhile, Miriam D. Rosenthal, a research fellow in
nutrition at Harvard's School of Public Health, has written a
bitter denunciation of Wilson and his associates, in which she
says: "Sociobiology, by encouraging biological and genetic
explanations for racism, war and genocide, exonerates and
protects the groups and individuals who have carried out and
benefited from these monstrous crimes. Proclaiming fascist-like
behavior as part of the 'human biogram,' it can only regard anti-
fascist behavior as an 'exception' which confirms a universal
human nature.... "

Then, as if to indict the university for playing a vanguard role
in promoting similar ideologies in former years, she alludes to the
fact that Harvard's President Eliot, immediately after his
appointment in 1869, invited John Fiske to deliver a series of
special lectures to promote Spencer's doctrine of "Social Dar-
winism." And just prior to World War I, then emeritus President
Eliot helped found the Race Betterment Foundation, a eugenics-
promoting organization on which he served as a member of its
central committee.

But in the final analysis, Ms. Rosenthal acknowledges that
thousands of Harvard students and faculty members have
traditionally opposed doctrines that encourage any form of
racism or class superiority.

Unfortunately, the widely publicized furor over sociobiology
has obscured the possibly more important contributions of other
scientists at Harvard, who for many years have profoundly
influenced the socioeconomic policies of private and governmental organization. Individually and jointly, they have produced basic research and theories that have served as the basis for
food and drug laws, medical care, weather forecasting, old-age

assistance, increased food production, educational reform, computer programming, psychiatric care, etc.—an infinite variety of programs that affect the daily lives of people all over the world. More than thirty years ago, for example, Professor Fred Whipple devised an imaginative and complex formula for computing interstellar gravitation, enabling astronomers to trace the trajectory and speed of thousands of stars and satellites. At any given moment, they could compute the exact position of a given star within infinite fractions of time and space. Thus, many years later, Whipple's formulas were an essential factor in the moon landing of American astronauts. And in the words of a fellow astrophysicist, "Even the Russian astronauts had to depend on Whipple's original computations, since Fred's brain is an international asset."

Of more earthly concern is the work of Professor Robert Woodward, the Harvard chemist who won the Nobel Prize in 1965 for his research in "synthetic organic chemistry." With enormous patience and skill, Woodward has isolated and identified the specific chemical properties of "natural products" such as quinine, patulin, cholesterol, cortisone, lanosterol, lysergic acid, strychnine, chlorophyll, tetracyclines and many other compounds. Needless to say, his findings have been used by thousands of companies who produce chemical compounds throughout the world. They have also enabled the U.S. Food and Drug Administration to impose stricter controls for the benefit of millions of consumers and medical patients.

Harvard men have also had considerable influence in the field of mathematics. In "numbers theory," Professors Barry Masur and John Tate have plowed new ground and earned the praise of fellow theorists. And Professors H. Hironaka and David Mumford have been equally successful in the more esoteric aspects of geometry. According to many of their colleagues, any one of these four scholars would be candidates for a Nobel Prize—but, unfortunately, there is no such award for mathematics. And the reason for this curious omission is all too human if not logical: Alfred B. Nobel specifically and irrevocably decreed that not one penny of his endowment would be used for an award in mathematics—and his motives were clear and simple: his wife had been openly and notoriously seduced by a world-famous Swedish mathematician. "It's comforting to know that old-fashioned jealousy affects even the greatest and richest of men," observed one Harvard intellectual. "But he need not have projected his spite into perpetuity."

Aside from the numerous and varied contributions of its faculty, Harvard has spread its influence far beyond the immediate environs of Cambridge. Hundreds of industrial firms and scientific laboratories, private and public, have managerial or technical personnel trained by the university's distinguished and demanding professors, many of whom have channeled their favorite graduate into strategic jobs throughout the world, thus casting their web of influence into all levels of scientific endeavor. "It's so damned incestuous," complained a biochemist from a midwestern university. "First of all, some Harvard guy works his way into a top position at some laboratory—and pretty soon his whole department is filled with people recommended by one of his old profs. So if you're not part of the club, that's tough shit, brother. But I guess I'd do the same thing—hire guys from my old school—except that you might get someone who's better trained if you get a Harvard man. At least that's the general impression in our line of work: it's either Harvard, MIT, Caltech, Stanford or Berkeley—but Harvard's the one you think about first."

And this incestuous web is perhaps more apparent in academia. Hundreds of university science professors throughout the United States (and numerous foreign countries) have graduate degrees from Harvard, many of them chairmen of departments "that seem to have been dredged from the Charles River," according to one indignant biology professor who earned his graduate degree at Michigan State. "Having failed to get tenure at dear old Harvard, they desparingly jumped into the chilly waters of the Charles, from which they've immediately been salvaged and then obsequiously idolatrized by other universities who still think that Harvard turds are minted gold."

But, if recent reports are any indication, Harvard-trained scientists may be experiencing a bit more difficulty in their quest for faculty positions on other campuses. One very promising biochemist, who failed to get tenure at Harvard despite high recommendations from a Nobel Prize winner, has solemnly confided to friends, "The Harvard mystique ain't what it used to be. The doors aren't as wide open—and there seem to be a lot fewer doors. There is probably a backlash against us—and, quite frankly, I'm not surprised."

Informed of this man's job-finding travails, a Columbia professor merely shrugged. "The job market is tight for everybody. But I would seriously doubt that Harvard men are suffering more than anyone else. They are simply more pampered and ego-inflated, so that even the slightest pinprick feels like mortal stab."

Harvard University's Hasty Pudding Club honored its 25th annual woman of the year yesterday, presenting Valerie Harper (television's Rhoda Morgenstern) with a bouquet of rhododendrons and putting her in a 1948 Lincoln limousine for a motorcade around Harvard Yard. She is the first television actress ever chosen by the theatrical club. Miss Harper, a graduate of Jersey City's Lincoln High School, said she always considered Harvard "big stuff."

—Laurie Johnston,
*The New York Times*

# CHAPTER XII Machismo—Eccentrics —Special Fellows

ALEKSANDR SOLZHENITSYN'S much-heralded speech at Harvard reminded certain alumni of a commencement ceremony shortly after World War II, when three distinguished generals— George Marshall, Omar Bradley and George Patton—were awarded honorary degrees on an afternoon that was memorable for at least two reasons:

First of all, General Marshall (newly appointed secretary of state) made a speech in which he outlined a detailed plan for massive economic-recovery aid for war-ravaged Europe—a proposal that was instantly dubbed the Marshall Plan.

Second, and perhaps more memorable to those present, the graduation exercises were preceded by the most colorful display of machismo one could possibly imagine. As the perspiring hordes of undergraduates and alumni pushed through Harvard Square toward the iron gates of the Yard, a screeching police siren drew their attention to a motorcycle-escorted military jeep moving along Massachusetts Avenue at a pace slow enough to assure everyone a good chance to see who was coming. And there, proudly perched on top of the back seat of the jeep, was General Patton fully attired in his battle uniform—his plastic white helmet gleaming in the sun, his medals and campaign ribbons dazzling the eye, his legendary pearl-handled pistols braced on his hips fully ready for a High Noon encounter in Harvard Square. No macho peacock had ever strutted so proudly, so grandly, so completely in command.

Yet there was a hint of self-mockery in his eyes as he acknowledged the waves and shouts and appreciative chuckles of a student body that had always delighted in elaborate deadpan put-ons.

Moments later, as the Patton entourage moved through the main gate of the Yard and into the quadrangle, he caught the attention of Generals Marshall and Bradley, both wearing modest civilian garb.

"Here comes George," said Marshall, unable to suppress a grin. "Ready for battle."

"Well, one thing you've got to say for him," said Bradley, shaking his head like the father of an unruly but charming child. "He's always himself."

"He sure is," said Marshall, "even at Harvard."

A somewhat different perspective was offered by a Radcliffe College graduate student, who neither applauded nor smiled when Patton went by. "That's the most disgusting macho stunt I've ever seen," she said to a male friend. "Not even Hemingway could top this one. But then Harvard is the perfect place for this kind of stuff—it's the most macho school in the country."

"Oh come off it, Liz," said her companion. "This is strictly a put-on: Patton is obviously laughing at his own image, and you're taking it seriously. You're always looking for something to stick at Harvard."

"So you don't think it's macho?"

"Well, *you're* studying here, Liz. Taking the same courses I am, the same goddam profs."

"But you're getting a Harvard Ph.D., and I'm getting mine

from Radcliffe. And to the world outside that's a big difference. So come off that crap!"

She was right, of course. She had more than sufficient reason to resent Harvard for its rank discrimination against her and every other woman—an institutionalized and outright discrimination that had persisted for more than three centuries. Not until fairly recently has this last bastion of male exclusivity given way to female demands for equal education. But even to this day, with their apparent full access to any and all university facilities, the undergraduate female students are still regarded as "Cliffies," though their diplomas are from Harvard. Female graduate students (law, medicine, etc.) have for several years received Harvard degrees, but are still a minority.

In any event, their current status is far more tolerable than the one forced upon Mathilda "Tilly" Holzman some thirty years ago. Possessed of a remarkable and imaginative intelligence, she was one of the very few graduate students who could grasp the most abstruse and subtle nuances of the mathematical economics then coming into vogue among Harvard's more advanced economists. Yet in the final showdown, she was never given the status routinely accorded to male students less brilliant than she. On the morning of her oral examinations, for example, she met an old friend near Harvard Square and asked him to walk her around the Yard to settle her nerves. Then, after a half-hour of idle chatter, she led him out of the main gates and across Massachusetts Avenue.

"Where are you going?" he asked, halfway across the avenue. "Aren't you supposed to take your orals in Emerson Hall?"

"Of course not," she said. "I'm being examined at Radcliffe College."

"That's absurd," he said. "All your courses have been at Harvard. You haven't taken a single damn course at Radcliffe."

"Well, I'm still considered a Cliffie," she said, "And that's where my doctorate will come from. So I've got to go through this formal charade of being examined at the college."

A few days later, one of her three examiners (all male Harvard professors) told one of his colleagues that Tilly's oral examination had been "the most impressive I've heard in the last fifteen years."

As further evidence of her academic excellence, Professor Wasily Leontief (generally considered the world's most brilliant economic theorist and later a Nobel Prize winner) asked Tilly to be his research and teaching assistant. But she was unable to accept the proffered appointment because her husband had been offered a position on the economics faculty at the University of Washington. And because of the ancient tradition that forbids a husband and wife from teaching in the same department, she switched fields and got a Ph.D. in psychology. Her husband, Frank Holzman, is now chairman of the economics department at Tufts University, where she also teaches child psychology, having recently spent a year as a research fellow at Harvard's prestigious Center for Cognitive Studies.

Had it not been for the academic machismo of that not-so-long-ago era, she most probably would have become a full professor at Harvard and a top-rank economist.

There *are* a few female professors at the university now, but some of them must suffer the all-too-macho suspicion that they achieved their status "the Hollywood way," i.e., by acquiring older male mentors more interested in their bodies than in their brains. "No matter how smart I am," says an attractive young teaching assistant, "my male competitors are sure to say that I've been shacking with the department chairman—and that horny old bastard has probably let them think so, even though I've politely asked him to keep his arthritic fingers off my fanny. But I'm told that a female professor in another department got tenure that way, so he probably expects the same fringe benefits—a sort of *droit de mentor*."

The mistress-mentor syndrome is a familiar phenomenon on campuses throughout the country, and there's no reason to believe that Harvard professors are immune, especially when one considers the drawing power of their special status. Perhaps when women have achieved equality (or even dominance) on college faculties, they too will demand a similar degree of sexual subservience from aspiring male protégés, or what might be called "erotic justice."

Progress in that direction has been dismayingly slow and fitful, and women too often conspire against their own interests. All too frequently, bright females conceal their intelligence and pretend to be ignorant and innocent on the assumption (unfortunately correct at times) that men fear intellectual competition. Even more troubling is the deep-seated sense of inferiority that so many women develop as a result of prolonged social conditioning. And this is true even among females with superior academic records. Mattina Horner, the president of Radcliffe College, has said that some very gifted female students often feel inferior in the presence of obviously average male Harvard students, that they seemed to be plagued by persistent expectations of failure. This seems particularly true in subjects traditionally considered beyond the grasp of a female brain—math, chemistry, biology, etc.

Going along with this self-fulfilling prophecy, many professors consciously use a double standard in rating their male and female students. "Sure I grade women differently," said one male professor of economics. "You can't really expect them to be equal to men. What's more, they expect concessions. It's mostly women who come in griping and demanding a higher grade."

One professor who had no worries about women demanding higher grades was the late Joseph Schumpeter, who gave A's to all female students. His reasoning was the very essence of male chauvinism: "Any young lady who has sense enough to take my course deserves an A."

## Eccentrics

Schumpeter's grading policy was considered somewhat eccentric by his more conventional colleagues; but compared to some of the professors and students at the university, he was only mildly eccentric. For Harvard, like Oxford, is a haven for eccentrics, where even the most extreme behavior is taken for granted and often encouraged.

Among the most endearing faculty members was the late Harry Wolfson, whose bookcases were so overloaded that his icebox was usually full of books and packets of notes for his lectures on medieval philosophy. Reared in the vanishing era of Eastern European Talmudic scholarship, he had emigrated to America and enrolled at Harvard in 1912, remaining there to teach several generations of students until his death in 1974. In a series of brilliant books, he persuasively argued that medieval thinkers who wrote in Latin, Greek, Arabic and Hebrew were all part of a single pan-cultural dialogue that began with the Jewish philosopher named Philo and ended with Spinoza, the Spanish Jew.

Wolfson spent much of his life in the musty stacks of Widener Library, but he also spent hundreds of getaway hours at the local movie theaters, avidly watching the innane plot twists of his favorite detective thrillers. On one particular afternoon, as he was watching a Humphrey Bogart movie, his secretary crept into the row behind him and whisperingly informed him that he was due to teach a graduate seminar at that very hour.

"I'm sorry to disturb you," she said as they rushed through the theater lobby, "but I knew you'd forgotten about your class."

"That's okay," he said. "I've already seen that movie four times."

Wolfson would undoubtedly have enjoyed the remark of an undergraduate as he left the Brattle Theatre on a recent evening: "Listen, Debby, when you've seen *The Maltese Falcon* seventy-three times, it's bound to seem a little stale."

Such an addiction would completely mystify the Harvard astrophysicist who had not seen a movie since his junior high school years. "I saw one of those silly-ass Ginger Rogers epics," he recently told a colleague's wife, "and I decided right there and then that movies were a waste of time." He apparently also decided that most people are a waste of time and has studiously avoided any human contacts that he himself has not initiated. He most zealously demands privacy in the early-morning hours, invariably eating breakfast alone in the kitchen alcove while his wife and only child quietly eat in the dining room. Even their most infrequent overnight guests must respect his breakfast *solo*, generally receiving a vague nod when they say good morning.

"It's been this way since we got married," his wife explained to a recent guest. "He has to have complete silence in the morning, because that's when he does his heaviest thinking, and he hates any kind of intrusion."

On the other hand, this same astrophysicist had an Argentine colleague who was probably the most gregarious person in Cambridge. Charming and extremely sociable, he would constantly accept invitations to dinner and would just as constantly arrive late by several hours. One evening in January he was to be the extra man at a very intimate sit-down dinner for three couples. The other guests arrived within ten or fifteen minutes of the appointed hour (7:00 p.m.), but Felix was nowhere to be seen...or heard. Finally, after heating and reheating her gourmet meal until it was practically spoiled, the hostess served dinner at 10:00 p.m., all the while apologizing for the absence of her honored guest. Just past midnight, the other three guests finally made their departure amid further apologies for the absent Argentinian.

Then, promptly at 1:30 a.m., as the two weary hosts were finally falling asleep, there was a loud knocking at their front door. Thinking it might be the police with bad news about Felix, they both jumped out of bed, hastily donned their robes and hurried to open the door. And there was Felix, a bright but somewhat apologetic smile on his eager face and a wilted bunch of flowers in his hand.

"I'm so sorry I am a bit late," he said, suddenly switching to

Spanish. *"Se me atravesó un asunto"* ("A little matter came up").

Obviously not realizing what time it was, he gladly accepted their perfunctory invitation to have a drink while the hostess once again heated the *coq au vin*, which he ate like a famished tramp as he told them about some new interstellar gravitational movements he had been computing earlier in the evening.

When he finally left at daybreak, the host smiled at his wife and said, "How in the hell can anyone expect Felix to be on time? What difference can a few hours mean to a man who is constantly thinking of millions of years?"

But compared to J. Arthur Greenwood, Felix was almost conventional. As anyone who knew him in Cambridge during the late '40s will testify, J. Arthur became a Harvard legend even before the end of his freshman year. His intellectual exploits and unpredictable behavior were topics of conversation among students and professors in every branch of the university— particularly among doctoral candidates, who soon realized that the sixteen-year-old genius was highly conversant even in their special fields of knowledge. Almost every weekend he would get invitations to seven or eight parties by graduate students anxious to show their guests "the brightest star in Harvard's glittering diadem."

Although most congenial, J. Arthur would occasionally become so absorbed in some private thought—perhaps an abstruse mathematical theorem or a problem in linguistics—that he would lapse into an inpenetrable silence, completely oblivious of his immediate environs. He might, in that frame of mind, wander into a friend's apartment, abstractedly fix himself a Dagwood sandwich, and leave without saying a word to anyone in the apartment. Once, after fixing his sandwich at the apartment of a law student, he sat by the window and leafed through two or three hundred pages of *Bouvier's Law Dictionary*, quickly absorbing the contents of each page in fractions of a minute. Then, after an hour or so of silent reading, he got up to leave with his half-eaten sandwich, saying to his friend, "Let me know when you get to 'contingent remainders,' Hank—I've got a pun about Fearne that you might like."

About eighteen months later, when Hank began studying Fearne's treatise on contingent remainders, he reminded J. Arthur about his offer and was told a delightful and very appropriate pun about Fearne in Elizabethan verse.

One very rainy night, while the same Hank was studying trusts, he heard a loud thumping at the door—and when he opened it, there was J. Arthur in a wet raincoat, his hair plastered down with rainwater, his tennis shoes completely soaked and dripping.

"Ho, my good Hank," he said. "I would'st wager thou hast seldom been visited on such a foul night by such a visage as this!"

"Verily, Arthur," said Hank, attempting to fall into his jargon. "May I relieve you of your garb."

"Then, *ipso facto*," he said, removing his raincoat and standing there in his jockey shorts and bare upper torso, "thou hast seldom seen a less attired visage on such a night."

"Verily, verily," said Hank, taken aback for a fleeting moment. "And whither goest thou in what is obviously considerable haste?"

"To the telegrapher," he said, "to let pater and mater know that I have just been asked to join some honored men in confraternity—they who chose to call themselves Phi Beta Kappa. But I would have you scan the note, my good Hanko, to see if I communicate aright."

He had, in fact, written the message in Boolean algebra, and Hank told him that he seriously doubted that anyone would decipher it. Some days later, J. Arthur complained that his parents had sent no congratulations, that they were "awfully damned blase." But when they later got to Cambridge for the award ceremony, his father said, "What in God's hell was that damned telegram about?"

"I thought David would decode it for you," said J. Arthur, referring to his younger brother. But David, with whom Arthur frequently corresponded in a variety of esoteric codes, had not been available when the telegram arrived—and the elder Greenwoods had tossed it into the waste basket thinking it was just another collegiate gag.

As one might have expected, J. Arthur eventually aroused the genetic ambitions of a beautiful graduate student of comparative literature, who had read about Isadora Duncan's unrealized wish to bear a child by George Bernard Shaw. (ID: "With my beauty and your brains, it should be a fantastic child." GBS: "But what if it has your brains and my looks?") With Isadora's plan in mind, Feliciana Leary launched an earnest, prolonged campaign to woo J. Arthur into her very inviting erotic clutches—but finally gave up.

"I guess he's too young and innocent," she told Hank with a sigh of wistful resignation. "Three or four times I thought I had him sexually mesmerized—ready to go—then he'd suddenly start talking about some creep named Planck and his damned quantum theory."

Feliciana, whose burnished auburn-red hair and long slender neck gave her the appearance of a Modigliani model, was equally unsuccessful in her attempt to get impregnated by the legendary Father R. J. Feeney, the brilliant irascible priest who captivated hundreds of Harvard and Radcliffe students in the late '40s and early '50s. A scholarly and eclectic Jesuit who could quote Freud as easily as Thomas Aquinas, Feeney was eventually defrocked and excommunicated for denouncing Cardinal Cushing as "a heretic" when the good cardinal suggested that even non-Catholics might get to heaven. However reactionary he might have been, Feeney drew undergraduates to the Newman Center like a pied piper, and a militant few remained with him long after his ignominious banishment from the church. And in all the furor, Feliciana's erotic strategems came to naught.

There have been several colorful clerics around Harvard, but few as memorable as Brother Blue, an imaginative, articulate black clergyman who preaches brotherly love in a singular fashion, mixing scripture with Shakespeare in his own inimitable way. Always dressed in bright-blue clothes, with spangles and ribbons that suggest a medieval court jester, he recites soliloquies from *Hamlet, Henry V,* or *Romeo and Juliet* with the sonorous splendor of a seasoned English actor, then suddenly switches to black-dialect interpretations of the same lines.

Shortly after the historic blizzard of 1978, Brother Blue stood on a huge mound of snow in Harvard Square and held a crowd of 500 spectators literally spellbound with a stunning rendition of *Hamlet.* After delivering the opening soliloquy in a resonant conventional English voice, he paused for a moment, smiled at the expectant crowd with a ghetto impishness, then proceeded to talk about "poor old Ham."

"That dude had himself a problem," he said. "The minute his ol' papa died, his mama starts messin' around with his uncle. That's right, man—his daddy's very own brother. Couldn't hardly wait to hop 'tween those sheets that Brother Bill called in-cest-you-us. Now you know that anything that sounds like *that* has got to be bad—real bad. But not that kinda *bad*, brother, I mean *bad* bad. So poor ol' Ham..."

Unfortunately, it's impossible to capture the essence of a Brother Blue performance on mere paper: one has to see and hear him in the flesh to fully appreciate his genius. Indeed, by the very nature of their unique behavior, most eccentrics defy adequate description. Suffice it to say that Harvard offers a hospitable ambience for such nonconformists.

And, like most universities, it has a high tolerance for the intramural feuds of faculty prima donnas, the oh-so-subtle malice that is often masked with professional courtesy as this or that professor elbows aside an old colleague in the never-ending struggle for power and status. "We have refined the doublecross into an exquisitely fine art," said one professor. "Your victim should hardly feel the shaft." Consequently, most of the malice and envy is expressed indirectly—almost always spoken and seldom written, for plausible denials must be available.

Rarely does one come across the forthrightness of Thomas Hearne, the acerbic Oxford don who crucified most of his fellow scholars in eleven volumes of diaries. His description of Professor Humphrey Wanley is a fair sample of his pithy judgments: "A very loose, debauched Man, kept Whores, was a very great Sot, & by that means broke to pieces his otherwise very strong Constitution."

## Special Fellows

In the status-conscious atmosphere of Cambridge, certain people will inevitably try to rank the various "fellows" in terms of intellectual prestige or power. Some will say that the junior fellows are the elite, others will select the Nieman fellows, still others may prefer the Kennedy or Loeb fellows. They are all distinguished and privileged groups with individual claims of superiority, but most knowledgeable observers would probably rate them in the following order:

*Junior fellows*: With respect to sheer intellect and prior academic accomplishment, this group of ten men and women are at the very top level. Selected from all disciplines (science, liberal arts, medicine, law, philosophy, etc.), the junior fellows are given a generous stipend for a year's study in any field they wish, with no course requirements and no examinations. Meeting regularly with each other for lunch or dinner, with or without senior faculty, they freely discuss any ideas that come to mind and often acquire new insights from specialists in another field.

Among the junior fellows for 1977–78 were: Peter R. Parham (biochemical immunology), who spent the year studying the molecules involved in the growth and differentiation of different classes of cells, including uncontrolled growth of tumors; Karen Rosenberg (Slavic languages and literature), who researched eighteenth-century Russian prose and poetry; David D. Weinrich (sociobiology), who investigated the extent to which family size and aspects of mating behavior of humans can be explained in terms of Darwinian adaptation; and Edward Witten (physics), who worked toward a better understanding of the elementary particle theory, specifically how quarks are bound together to form particles.

In previous years, the junior fellows have included McGeorge Bundy and Daniel Ellsberg, discussed in an earlier chapter.

*Nieman fellows*: When the militant white South African journalist Donald Woods incurred the wrath of his government and felt compelled to sneak out of his country in the dead of night, hundreds of newspapers and television stations proclaimed him an international hero. And within a few days of his heroic self-exile, Harvard invited him to come to Cambridge as a Nieman fellow—an honor he instantly accepted.

Some people felt that Harvard's quick move was rank opportunism, an obvious use of the university's mystique to attract a new celebrity, and a casual violation of the Nieman Foundation's cautious, year-long process for selecting its fellows.

Like Woods, most of the fellows are prominent journalists who have been invited to spend a year at the university, receiving their regular salaries and travel expenses while doing so. "It's a dream vacation," said a recent recipient. "I can attend any classes I wish, write a damn novel, or sit on my fat ass on the library steps ogling the Radcliffe girls. And I get paid exactly what I earned sweating out deadlines on my hometown newspaper."

They are also constantly wined and dined by professors who are attracted to reporters who have had firsthand exposure to wars, racial strife, Washington shenanigans and all the excitement that takes place in the "real world." And perhaps—just perhaps—the journalistic dinner guest may some day mention his host as a "world-renowned authority" on the sociobiological implications of the Middle East negotiations or whatever else has been discussed during predinner cocktails. And that may not be a vain hope when one considers the number of Nieman fellows who have won the Pulitzer Prize and written best-selling books on public affairs.

*Kennedy fellows*: Even more famous than the journalists are some of the politicians and public officials who become Kennedy fellows at the Institute of Politics. Senator Eugene McCarthy, Governor John Connally, HUD Secretary Robert Weaver and Mayor James Morrall (New Orleans) have been short-term fellows, while less-known government officials have been year-long fellows. Needless to say, many of these visiting political figures are wooed socially by professors and students alike, and their seminars often draw overflow audiences. (For further information on the Kennedy fellows, the Institute of Politics and its academic parent, the Kennedy School of Government, refer to Chapter IV.)

*Loeb fellows:* Fifteen urban planners, architects and ecologists have been selected yearly as Loeb fellows at the Harvard Graduate School of Design. Begun in 1970–71, this fellowship program honors persons with "exceptional promise" in the fields of urban affairs and design. Although generally from Massachusetts, some of the fellows come from foreign countries. The 1977–78 group, for example, included George McClure, director of urban planning and design, Centre d'Etudes Techniques de l'Equipement, Ministry of Public Works in France. In the words of a recent fellow, Alex Rodriguez of the Massachusetts Commission Against Discrimination, "Most of us had considerable experience in some aspect of public affairs, so that our discussions were seldom abstract or mere theory."

*Appointments:* Far more coveted than any of the aforementoned fellowships are two appointments: the Charles Eliot Norton Lecturer and the Godkin Lecturer. Perhaps the most celebrated Norton Lecturer was Leonard Bernstein, who occupied the post in 1973, during which he explored the possibility that all music might be based on a universal structure similar to the grammatical structure proposed by Noam Chomsky and other modern linguistic scholars. Bernstein's dazzling lectures to

Harvard students were filmed for public television and received extensive coverage and comment in the press media. One writer noted, "Mr. Bernstein, who is nothing if not a generalist, came in for much adverse criticism, not only from specialists who thought he was building his language theory out of false analogies and with generally discarded acoustical concepts, but also from those who automatically dismiss anything he says as pap for the middlebrow masses."

A more direct appraisal was voiced by a New York colleague: "Leonard's lectures were full of shit—even though he delivered them at Harvard."

Allen Keiler, in a subsequent issue of the *Music Quarterly*, evaluated the lectures as a bit confusing and unconvincing but nevertheless concluded, "The challenge that is sounded in Bernstein's lectures at Harvard is an important one in the study of music."

Whoever gives the Norton lectures usually gets considerable publicity, and the Harvard connection is always mentioned in the headline or lead paragraph as if to give added authority to whatever has been said. Among the past lecturers (mostly people from the creative arts) are Felix Candela, Frank Kermode, Northup Frye, I.M. Pei, and Robert Penn Warren.

The Godkin lectures are delivered by world-renowned authorities in the social sciences and political economy, among whom were Harold Laski, Frederick Hayek, Norbert Schlie, Charles Schultze, Elliot Richardson, Carl Kaysen and several U.S. cabinet members dating back to the Truman era.

### Harvard Lampoon

But of all the honorary citations that come from the university, the most notorious are the "Woman of the Year" and "Man of the Year" awards by the Hasting Pudding Club and the student humor magazine, the *Harvard Lampoon*. Selected with tongue in cheek, the recipients are generally from the entertainment world—preferably outrageous in their personal life-styles or unwitting caricatures of themselves. Among the more recent ones were Elizabeth Taylor, John Wayne, Chevy Chase, Bette Midler, Jack Lemmon, Rhoda (Valerie Harper), and Johnny Carson. Several years ago, Katherine Anne Porter was chosen and later said, "I loved every silly minute of my visit to Cambridge, especially the loony party in their crazy little castle."

The castle is an odd-shaped gothic building bearing a faint resemblance to William Randolph Hearst's castle in San Simeon—and well it should, for it was Hearst who donated the building to the magazine in fond remembrance of his old "poonie pals." Apparently all the awardees have enjoyed their crazily voluptuous receptions, especially Professor John Kenneth Galbraith—regarded by the poonies as a media personality—who was given a snazzy purple Cadillac sedan and $10,000 for being both witty and wise.

When Johnny Carson was chosen Man of the Year in 1977, he prefaced his visit to Cambridge with constant references to Harvard during his opening patter on the *Tonight Show* on three successive nights. Switching from his usual bantering put-downs of presidents and princesses alike, he seemed almost reverential as he talked to his straight man about "the greatness" of the university, about its "best faculty in the world," about all the great men it has produced. He was, in short, reinforcing the mystique for millions of televiewers. As one of his regular fans remarked to a fellow barroom spectator, "Jesus, old Johnny's gone fruit over Harvard, and he ain't even got there yet!"

When he did get there, Carson was treated lavishly and with ill-disguised reciprocal reverence, for no one seems immune to theatrical celebrities—not even the most blasé poonie.

There are some *Lampoon* progeny who never seemed able to cut the umbilical cord, who wanted to remain poonies for the rest of their lives. Three of them—Douglas Kenney, Henry Beard and Robert Hoffman—graduated from college and immediately launched a magazine called the *National Lampoon*, which has become so successful that it has recently branched out into the motion-picture industry, producing a film called *Animal House*, a trifle about college pranksters, which turned into a financial bonanza. "The *Harvard Lampoon* was my 'animal house,'" Kenny later told a reporter. "I didn't want it to end, so I got Matty Simmons to make it a national magazine. Now, as I look back at the past decade, I see a group of about thirty people that I have worked with again and again. I expect to work with them for the next ten years. We were the generation that discovered alienation is funny. We found that if you take an existentialist, add a hot Camaro, a skateboard and a lot of dope, you have a working, vital existentialist who can get a job at the *National Lampoon*."

Not suprisingly, the more recent graduates of Harvard seem to be cut from a different mold. Here, for example, are the thoughtful musings of Kate Wenner in *The Village Voice*: from July 12, 1977:

Practically no student talked about Harvard as if he or she were actually a part of it. Even people who were insightful about how Harvard worked as an institution, bogged down completely in trying to explain their relationship to it. Students complained about the pressures to perform, the atmosphere of selfishness and intellectual arrogance. But when I asked why they didn't quit, they'd make jokes, or change the subject, or giggle in the most disarming way. Harvard has people hooked, not because of what it gives them as an experience, but because of what it represents in power and status and will give them in security and personal gain. Many in my generation had reacted to the double bind of an elite education by rebelling and buying out. These new students, this "new breed," are reacting to the same basic conflicts by affirming ambition and personal isolation and making an imperative of blindness. . . . Nelson Aldrich wrote in *Harper's* that the old elitism of upper-class New England at Harvard is on the wane. But it's being replaced by something more efficient, more intractable, more manageable, and also a lot harder to fight.

At Harvard, all they have to do is pick up the phone and six governors, eight U.S. Senators, at least two members of the Queen's Court and numerous other big people drop onto the front lawn. To most of them a place like Northeastern sounds like a wind direction instead of a school and to all of them Harvard sounds like power. On Friday and Saturday, Cambridge was filled with muscle as a long line of notables dropped by to help celebrate the 10th anniversary of the Kennedy Institute of Politics. What took place could qualify for the semifinals of the World Series of Boredom.

—Mike Barnicle,
*Boston Globe* columnist

CHAPTER XIII **Who Really Runs Harvard? The Power Behind the Power**

WHEN ABLADIF AL HAMAD, director of the multibillion-dollar Kuwait Fund for Arab Economic Development, visited the university two years ago, a graduate student smilingly speculated, "He's here to negotiate a price for the purchase of Harvard—only the Arabs have that much money."

Actually, al-Hamad was in Cambridge as a distinguished member of a Visiting Committee; but if he or any other sheik were to buy the university, they would be acquiring scores of new and ancient buildings, a vast amount of real estate on both sides of the Charles River, 190 libraries, the world's finest collection of glass flowers, three observatories, and a fairly large forest. But these are only the visible manifestations of Harvard's immense wealth: it also has huge holdings in stocks and bonds, as well as equities in nonacademic real estate—all of which constitute the largest endowment of any university in the world.

Such wealth, according to a local underground newspaper, underscores issues that have been hotly debated on campuses throughout the country. What moral compromises can a university accept in order to finance its scholastic operations?

[227]

Who should decide how to invest a school's endowment? How actively should a university attempt to influence the policies of corporations in which it has invested? Perhaps because it is the most heavily endowed, Harvard has been the focus of the most violent eruptions concerning these issues.

The first (and perhaps the most tumultuous) came on April 20, 1972, when thirty-five black students seized possession of Massachusetts Hall and the university president's office therein and staged a week-long demonstration protesting Harvard's considerable investment in Gulf Oil Company stock. Along with hundreds of white student and faculty supporters, the blacks insisted that Gulf was a main bulwark of the Portuguese colonial regime in Angola and that Harvard's $20 million equity in the company constituted an indirect support of imperialism. The university had previously resisted demands for divestiture and, in fact, had used its shareholder votes to endorse the company's policy of not publicizing its corporate activities in Angola. The students' much-publicized occupation failed to alter the university's investment policy, but President Bok nevertheless sought to assuage their anger by sending an aide to Angola to observe Gulf's operations. He also made a move that no doubt startled the old Bostonians who traditionally controlled the financial policies of the university: he created a tripartite Advisory Committee on Shareholder Responsibility, composed of four students, four faculty members and four alumni.

At the very outset, Bok's decision seemed like both a challenge and a threat to university administrators elsewhere, none of whom had ever admitted "student intrusion" into the sacred domain of investment policy. But they—like the aforementioned Bostonians—soon realized that the threatened intrusion was mostly illusory, that the ACSR membership was topheavy with conservative Brahmin corporate directors and circumspect business and law professors—so that the student contingent, however radical it might be, could have little or no real influence. Moreover, the committee's power was merely *advisory*. The ultimate authority still rested with the Harvard Corporation, the school's traditionally conservative governing board.

Aware of student accusations that ACSR was "just an appeasement gambit," its executive secretary defended his committee as a viable conduit for student grievances "which could lead to further disruptions if left unchanneled." He further disputed the charge that big business was overrepresented on the ACSR, noting that while the four alumni representatives were corporate executives, the faculty and student members would serve on a rotating basis so as to guarantee an expression of university-wide sentiments.

One alumni representative, Guido Perera, an executive with Welch & Forbes, insisted that there was a "substantial exchange of views" at committee meetings and that the business-oriented members were perfectly willing to discuss moral issues and to question whether certain companies in which Harvard has investments "are good corporate citizens."

But whatever the outcome of such inquiries, the recommendations of the ACSR must be reviewed and accepted or rejected by a four-man subcommittee of the all-powerful Harvard Corporation, which then decides how the university will vote its shares at corporate stockholder meetings. (One should bear in mind, however, that most stockholder meetings are prearranged *pro forma* exercises in which the prior decisions of the controlling administration are automatically ratified. Thus, if Harvard's shares are minimal, its voice will get polite but scant attention.) As for the recommendations of the advisory committee, the record suggests only moderate success. In April 1978, the ACSR suggested: (1) that Harvard vote against letting Manufacturers Hanover Trust accede to the Arab boycott of Israeli-connected firms; (2) that it vote against permitting Union Carbide to dig a new mine in South Africa; and (3) that it vote for allowing the more progressive Texaco Corporation to stay in South Africa. The seven members of the corporation unanimously accepted all three recommendations.

Their reactions to three other suggestions by the ACSR were decidedly different. As to the committee's advice that Harvard vote to have General Electric withdraw its operations from South Africa, the corporation decided to abstain on the question, asserting that GE was a "responsible employer" and preferable to whatever European company might take its place. With respect to the ACSR recommendation that Harvard vote for a proposed resolution that Mobil Oil forbid its subsidiaries from selling oil to Rhodesia, the corporation once again chose to abstain, stating that the laws governing foreign corporations in that region were unclear as to Mobil's choice of customers. As to the advisory committee's suggestion that Harvard urge Gulf Oil to amend its articles of incorporation so as to prohibit its executives from bribing foreign leaders, the corporation later voted against such an amendment. In response to a reporter's query, Hugh Calkins, Chairman of the Harvard Corporation's subcommittee on shareholder responsibility, simply explained, "We don't believe Gulf will make illegal payoffs in the future."

When one considers the big-business involvements of the university's governing board, such an affirmation of unquestioning faith in "one's own kind" is not at all surprising. The self-elected, self-perpetuating members of the elite Harvard Corporation have always been "men of substance," men with extensive ties to the upper levels of industry and finance. Most of them have served on the board of directors (or trustees) of numerous corporations, generally those listed as the top 400 on the *Fortune* magazine roster. Often possessed of inherited wealth and inclined toward the quiet, unspectacular ethos of the "old Bostonian," they have studiously avoided the limelight and are thus virtually unknown outside the ambit of the chosen few. To the average jet-setter, a George Putnam or a Hugh Calkins would be nonentities—and they might also be unknown to the flamboyant millionaires of the great southwest—but on Wall Street their names would be instantly recognized and respected.

To a lesser degree, the same would be true of those who serve on the Board of Overseers, who also exercise some degree of authority on matters of broader scope. With a more diverse mix of notables, the board now includes a few blacks and women; but its membership is still largely composed of such past and present establishment figures as Averell Harriman, John F. Kennedy, Douglas Dillon, David Rockefeller, Roswell Gilpatric, Andrew Heiskell, Joseph Pulitzer and Walter Rothschild.

Although the corporation (sometimes referred to as "the President and Fellows") have the final say on the university's financial policy, the actual day-to-day decisions are made by the Harvard Management Company. One should note, incidentally, that the university gets 20% of its annual income from investment dividends, 30% from student tuitions, 24% from government contracts and grants, 15% from gifts, and the remaining 11% from real-estate rentals and miscellaneous sources. The task of investing the school's huge endowment belongs to HMC, which is unique among "investment houses" in that its nine senior analysts handle just one account. Most other universities assign this responsibility to their treasurer or outside managers, and some pool their resources in an investment group known as the Common Fund. A few, such as Yale, use brokerage firms of which they are part owners. Only Harvard, perhaps by necessity, has set up its own seemingly autonomous company to handle its enormous fortune.

When one includes the university's real-estate holdings at book value (usually very low) and subtract obligations under secured lending agreements, Harvard's "General Investment Account" totaled $1,427,926,795 as of June 30, 1976. Approximately 60% of this sum was invested in common stocks, convertible bonds and convertible preferred stock. The balance consisted of cash deposits, other bonds, mortgages, loans and real estate. And this overall investment has usually netted Harvard a rather respectable return of 11.8% per year at a time when other investors have been biting their nails.

But the investment philosophy of HMC is not altogether

acceptable to certain faculty members and students. Their negative feelings were reflected by an editorial critic who raised the issue of morality in the *Real Paper*:

Though HMC head Walter Cabot claims to be "very sensitive to the moral problems of investing," most evidence suggests that Harvard values profit over conscience. A three-page description of HMC in the university's financial report boasts that the investment firm can "focus on such broad issues as world-wide economic, political and sociological trends" and "form sound opinions on international problems, especially regarding fuel and food supplies." The passage avoids any explicit mention of ethical factors in investment decisions. Cabot himself says he "won't duck a company if it's attractive" just because some of its operations seem distasteful. He cites the example of Dow Chemical, a company in which Harvard has invested more than $12 million. Napalm's being one of Dow's products is outweighed, Cabot says, by the many good commodities the company makes and by its sure profitability.

About 25% of the 200 corporations in Harvard's investment portfolio are listed in the *Directory of American Firms Operating in Foreign Countries* as having subsidiary plants or sales offices in South Africa. Since most of these firms are long-established and very profitable multinational conglomerates, HMC's investments in them are disproportionately larger than investments in moderate-sized businesses elsewhere. In fact, the market value of the university's shareholdings in these South African-connected companies is in excess of $565 million, almost 40% of its total endowment. Even though Harvard's equity in corporations such as General Electric, ITT, General Motors, Union Carbide, Kodak, Exxon, Mobil, IBM and Kimberly-Clark has provoked angry criticism from the Committee Against Racism and the student newspaper (the *Crimson*), there has been only minimal concern from the public at large.

But in the spring of 1978 the issue flared anew when hundreds of students once again invaded the administration offices and staged an all-night vigil around Massachusetts Hall, demanding divestiture in all companies doing business in South Africa. There were candlelit parades through the Yard and strident speeches around Harvard Square; but, after several days pondering the issues, the Harvard Corporation courteously announced that it sympathized with student demands and abhorred the apartheid policies of South Africa—but that it could be more effective in advocating change by retaining its shares in the disputed companies.

The following list of the university's major investments was prominently displayed by the protestors and subsequently published in one of the local newspapers:

## HARVARD INVESTMENTS
### The Top 40

| | |
|---|---|
| U.S. government | $246,914,156 |
| IBM | 74,190,498 |
| Ford | 55,562,975 |
| Mobil | 53,036,556 |
| Exxon | 41,937,361 |
| Quebec Hydro-Electric | 31,354,629 |
| GM | 30,614,761 |
| Eastman Kodak | 26,828,948 |
| Continental Oil | 22,064,320 |
| General Reinsurance Group | 21,790,981 |
| MAPCO | 21,218,851 |
| Getty | 20,219,903 |
| Atlantic Richfield | 17,570,839 |
| Standard Oil of California | 17,074,654 |
| St. Regis Paper | 15,353,397 |
| General Electric | 15,187,405 |
| Sears, Roebuck | 14,924,906 |
| Beneficial | 13,822,884 |
| Caterpillar Tractor | 13,741,103 |
| Province of Ontario | 12,335,910 |
| Dow Chemical | 12,227,949 |

| Aluminum Co. of America | 11,865,565 |
| Union Carbide | 11,068,724 |
| U.S. Steel | 10,915,154 |
| Kimberly-Clark | 10,676,454 |
| International Nickel of Canada | 10,502,593 |
| Proctor, Gamble | 10,376,375 |
| Continental Group | 9,939,553 |
| SmithKline | 8,946,986 |
| Phillips Petroleum | 8,918,217 |
| Standard Oil of Indiana | 8,913,351 |
| Dome Petroleum | 8,635,656 |
| Gulf | 8,538,075 |
| Pennzoil | 8,280,000 |
| Kingdom of Norway | 8,072,510 |
| Bristol-Myers | 7,493,988 |
| Johnson and Johnson | 7,474,908 |
| Texaco | 7,463,485 |
| Federated Department Stores | 7,200,423 |
| Georgia-Pacific | 6,969,340 |

As the students marched around President Bok's office, chanting his name and demanding that he sell the "tainted stock," a young professor wearily remarked to a female companion: "What's the use of all this demonstrating? Bok won't give in, and we all know it. After all, he wasn't elected to preside over the liquidation of this empire."

# Conclusion

WHEN S.I. HAYAKAWA told me that he had always been bugged by the mystique of Harvard, "even though I know there are as many silly asses there as anywhere else," he was very clearly expressing the sentiments of thousands of well-educated Americans, many of whom view Harvard with an admixture of awe and resentment.

The resentment is all too frequently justified by the smugness and arrogance of many Harvard graduates and/or by their incestuous tendency to promote each other in preference to outsiders who may be equally or more capable.

The awe is more difficult to assess because it is so often based on exaggeration, on fiction rather than fact, on an accumulation of myths, many of which have been created by people who have never been at Harvard. Novelists, magazine editors, news columnists and screenwriters have repeatedly used the Harvard label to connote power, wealth, super intelligence and snobbery, so that their readers and audiences are led to believe that the university produces nothing but geniuses with a guaranteed access to the best jobs, best salaries, best clubs and best women or men.

Given that mystique, one can easily understand why some people happily note even the slightest decline in the prestige and influence of "dear old Harvard." Just recently a UCLA professor pointedly remarked that Jimmy Carter's administration was doing quite well without a Cambridge mafia. But when he was reminded that Harvard men direct the National Security Council, HEW, the Department of Energy and the Domestic Council and also serve as solicitor general and secretary of the army, he unhesitatingly quipped, "No wonder Carter is in such bad shape—he's got the least and the lightest."

Although I admire the professor's clever allusion to Halberstam's *The Best and the Brightest*, I would disagree with both extremes of his ambivalent attitude, for there is neither an absence nor an excess of Harvard influence in the present administration. Indeed, the university's impact on President Carter has been less than it was on Nixon, Johnson, Kennedy, Truman or Roosevelt. Whether this has been good or bad for the country, only history will tell—but there is an increasing number of knowledgeable people who confidently feel that a new wave of Harvard men and women will soon gush into Washington, and the reason for their confidence is the growing expectation that Senator Edward M. Kennedy will succeed Carter in 1980. Even now, eighteen months before the next presidential campaign, there is considerable talk around Cambridge about a new Kennedy administration, a sense of anticipation among those who participated in the mythic Camelot of the older brother, and among the younger professors and graduate students who are eager to build a new Camelot.

But aside from politics and public affairs, one may wonder about the extent of Harvard's influence in other aspects of our daily lives. There is, of course, no way of measuring the influence of any single institution, but it is obviously substantial. And if one is to judge from newspaper headlines, magazine articles, novels, television commentaries and movies like *Love Story* and *Paper Chase*, one may safely assume that the Harvard mystique has not diminished—and that those who either hate the university or love it will have much to quote for their respective bias. Those who love it will no doubt wish to quote the aforementioned answer of Aleksandr Solzenhitzyn when he was asked why he had chosen to speak at Harvard after rejecting hundreds of invitations from other universitities: "Because Harvard is Harvard," he said.

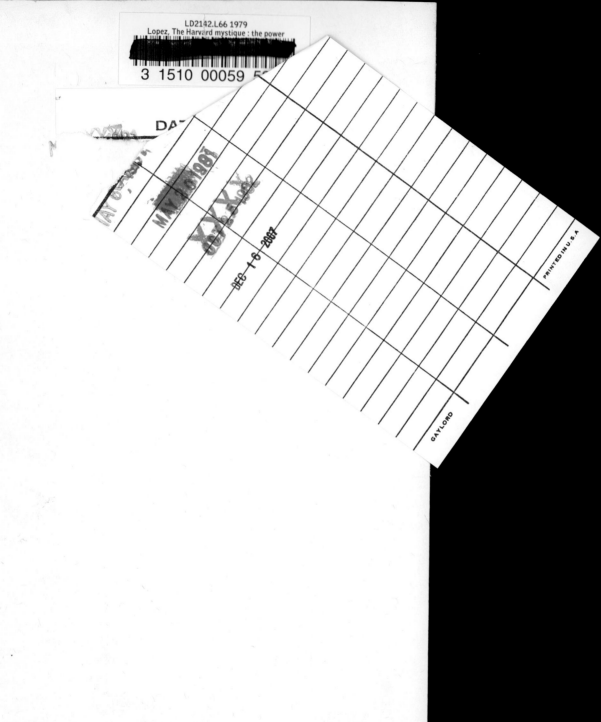